D0843045

Ernesto Laclau

NLB

Politics and Ideology in Marxist Theory

Capitalism – Fascism – Populism

First published by NLB, 1977

Second impression, 1979
NLB, 7 Carlisle Street, London W1

Printed in Great Britain by
Lowe & Brydone Printers Limited, Thetford, Norfolk

ISBN 86091 714 2 (paper)
ISBN 902308 74 2 (cloth)

Contents

To Chantal

Introduction

Men who, since childhood, have had their backs to the entrance of a cave, cannot see the outside world. On the wall inside the cave are projected the shadows of other men, and by linking the voices of these men to their shadows, the inhabitants of the cave conclude that the first derive from the second. One of the prisoners, however, manages to escape and perceives the true origin of the voices. Finally he emerges from the cave and sees the light of day. At first the sun blinds him, but then he becomes accustomed to it and the vision he gains enables him to understand the falsehood in which he had been living.

Plato's allegory of the cave contains for the first time in history a *theory of articulation*. Common sense discourse, *doxa*, is presented as a system of misleading articulations in which concepts do not appear linked by inherent logical relations, but are bound together simply by connotative or evocative links which custom and opinion have established between them. It is precisely the systematic character of this ensemble of articulations which Plato's intervention tries to break: in the Dialogues the unity of common sense discourse (what we would call today ideological discourse) is dissolved by a critical process which leads to the 'purification' of each concept. The critique consists in the breaking of those links between concepts which are the mere residue of opinion and custom. For beyond their connotative relationships, these concepts display an essential paradigmatic coherence to which the privileged vision of the philosopher leads. Knowledge presupposes, then, an operation of rupture: a disarticulation of ideas from those connotative domains to which they appear linked in the form of a misleading necessity, which enables us subsequently to reconstruct their true articulations.

This dual movement – a rupture of the apparent obviousness of articulations established by custom, and an attempt to discover essential paradigmatic relations by means of a simple analysis of concepts – has long constituted a characteristic and constant feature of European thought. From the 'methodological vagrancy' of Descartes to the appeal to the 'noble savage' of the 18th century, or the Enlightenment quest in Persia or China for paradigms critical of the existing social order, European thought was increasingly to use confrontations between different cultures as a means of relativizing its own institutions, customs and habits of thought. Thereby those concepts which defined for the bourgeoisie the abstract conditions of any possible society, lost their necessary articulation with the concrete forms in which those conditions were locally materialized. This was the case, for example, with the decline of absolutism as a hegemonic ideology in Europe. The defence of the existing social order, of private property and other principles identified by the bourgeoisie with the very existence of the community, appeared less and less linked to the institution of monarchy: the identification between the two, which had constituted the core of the political discourse of absolutism, began to dissolve, like the relation between the voices and the shadows in Plato's cave. It was possible after a certain point to be conservative without being monarchical, although to break the bond between the two principles and transform this rupture into an obvious fact of political discourse required, in France, more than a century. In the same way, it took a long time for the concept of 'organized economic community' to be articulated within the dominant ideological discourse, with the basic principles of economic liberalism. Adam Smith's 'invisible hand' was anything but evident for his contemporaries. Finally, to extricate the concept of democracy from the negative connotations of 'mob-rule' and transform it into a positive concept increasingly articulated with liberal political discourse, demanded the whole alternating process of revolutions and reactions throughout the nineteenth century.

These successive attempts to break the 'ideological' articulations of discourse undoubtedly led to an increasing 'purification' of concepts in Europe. Classical political economy arose from this process of abstraction, as did political theory based on the notion of contract. However, the progressive divorce between the abstract character of concepts and the ideological-connotative domain to which they had hitherto been articulated, led in time to an opposite illusion: the supposition that, beyond common sense discourse, concepts separated from any connotative articulation could, by a simple exposition of their logical qualities, reconstruct reality as a whole. This was the rationalist ambition that runs through Western philosophy from Plato to Hegel. If the level of *doxa* constitutes a continuous fabric which absorbs and articulates every possible meaning, the level of philosophy aspires to reconstruct the totality of this fabric *in a necessary order and through rational links*. Indeed at its apogee, philosophical knowledge tried to absorb Platonic dualism: for Hegel, appearance is a moment of essence. Reabsorbed as a moment of essence in the Hegelian dialectic or crystallized as the pole of an irreducible dualism in the Platonic dialectic, the connotative articulations of discourse constituted the antagonistic point of reference against which philosophy tried to reconstruct concepts *in themselves*. If at the level of *doxa* concepts appear articulated by formal principles external to their logical nature, philosophy made their logical properties the only principles relating them as concepts. It further postulated the systematic character of these relations, and the possibility of reconstructing through them a system as broad as that which had characterized the discourse of *doxa*. This was the process whereby concepts were to be rearticulated on the basis of their essential cohesion within a paradigm. The whole effort of disarticulation was therefore only the prologue to the postulation of necessary paradigmatic linkages. The result was that when a relativism later developed, which renounced paradigms and limited intellectual endeavour to a description of various articulations historically *given*, the inevitable accompaniment was a growing scepticism about knowledge as such.

What happens, on the other hand, if we accept a scientific approach and keep as the essential task of theoretical practice the 'purification' of concepts – that is to say the elimination of any connotative articulations – whilst asserting the impossibility of rearticulating them into necessary paradigmatic wholes? Three essential consequences follow from this change of view. Firstly, not every concept has a necessary relation with others. It is not possible, therefore, starting with only one of them, to reconstruct the totality of the system. Systematic wholes, in other words, depend on the articulation of concepts which are not logically inter-linked. Secondly, it is not possible to establish necessary relations between different conceptual structures – such that we could pass from one to the other by a purely deductive process – but only the conditions of possibility of their articulation. Thirdly, therefore, any approximation to the concrete presupposes increasingly complex conceptual articulations and not the mere exposition of the logical properties of a simple conceptual whole. Consequently, the more concrete is the analysis, the more theoretical determinations must be included in it; and since theoretical determinations are not necessary moments in the self-unfolding of an essence but discrete conceptual formations, the precondition for any theoretical approximation to the concrete comprises a progressive process of abstraction which frees concepts from their connotative articulations.

Theoretical practice has been greatly hindered by the two obstacles we have discussed: the connotative articulation of concepts at the level of common sense discourse and their rationalist articulation into essential paradigms. The essays in this volume have been written in the conviction that these obstacles have combined to create an unsatisfactory state of affairs for Marxist theory. They have also been written in the conviction that the most recent Marxist thought, from Della Volpe to Althusser, has started to construct the conditions for a scientific reading of Marxism that will enable us to overcome these critical difficulties. To see how this combination of obstacles has operated, let us look at the problem of the connotative articulations of ideological discourse. To the extent that Marxist theoretical practice has been historically linked to socialist political practice, connotative articulations of political discourse have tended to be automatically transformed into theoretical determinations. Take, for example, the concept of 'capitalist'. In Marxist theory this concept has a defined theoretical status: it is one of the poles of the relation of production constituting the capitalist mode of production. Now the agents which are the bearers of this structural relation are at the same time the points of intersection of a multiplicity of relations and contradictions articulated by class practices. In political discourse, therefore, it is not the 'capitalist as such' which is present but concrete capitalists, or to put it another way, the theoretical determination of 'capitalist' is *connotatively* linked to a complex of other theoretical determinations. It is only a short step from here to suppose that 'capitalist' is not a *theoretical concept* but the *name* of the agent, and that as such it alludes to the ensemble of its determinations and not just to one of them. Therewith, we unite once again the voices and the shadows. Any of the features of this new synthetic subject, the 'capitalist', will then be evocative or indicative of the totality of them. One might think that this is an ideological effect of political discourse, which theoretical practice can promptly clear away. But at this point the other obstacle intervenes: the postulation of paradigmatic relations. Traditionally, among the various paradigms which have characterized the kind of Marxism with which we are concerned, there is one which is the source of them all: class reductionism. Contradictions are seen in a hierarchical system that can be directly or indirectly reduced to a class contradiction. Any element or contradiction at the political and ideological level is, therefore, a class appurtenance. The paradoxical result is that theoretical practice has no need to correct the connotative articulations of political discourse, because if all political and ideological determinations have a necessary class ascription, they are also therefore expressive of the class essence of the subject. Since all of them, taken individually, express this subject equally, concretization of analysis can then only consist of the progressive unfolding of this essence.

The great problem for this approach is how theoretically to analyze pertinent differences – how, for example, to render class reductionism compatible with the actual historical variety of bourgeois ideologies. The usual solutions have been either to regard differences as simply *accidental* (so that they are not theoretically conceived at all) or to explain them in terms of a distinct *level of development* reached by a mode of production (capitalism in the ascendant was expressed by liberalism, capitalism in decline by fascism, and so on). We do not wish to examine here the various expedients whereby class reductionism has tried to integrate historical variety into its schema – some of them are studied and criticized elsewhere in this volume. What is important to emphasize is that the efficacy of these expedients has been gradually reduced as the historical experience of the class struggle and the ascent of the masses on a world scale has progressively broken down the system of connotative articulations in which the provincial Eurocentrism of the Second and Third Internationals had encapsulated Marxist theoretical concepts. Not for nothing did the Althusserian endeavour arise in a world dominated by the division of the world communist movement, by the end of the cold war, by decolonization and by the emergence of new contradictions in advanced capitalist countries. The magnitude of the theoretical and political problems confronting Marxism in this new historical situation necessitated a rupture with the last traces of reductionism. The abandonment of the Platonic cave of class reductionism demands, today, an increasing theoretical formalization of Marxist categories, breaking at once with the connotative articulations of political discourse and with the postulation of paradigmatic relations between concepts. This enterprise can in turn only be beneficial for socialist political practice, at a time when the proletariat must abandon any narrow class perspective and present itself as a hegemonic force to the vast masses seeking a radical political reorientation in the epoch of the world decline of capitalism. This is the domain where Marxism in the last two decades has made undeniable advances, and it is to this task that the essays presented here are intended to make a modest contribution.

The four essays which follow have a similar structure. All of them start from one or more theoretical concepts and certain polemics that have developed over them. They then seek to demonstrate the way in which confusions have arisen, either through a failure to respect the level of abstraction of the concept in question by introduction of theoretical determinations appropriate only to more concrete levels of analysis, or through a denial of the specificity of a determinate contradiction and an assimilation of it to another in a reductionist fashion. In the case of the polemic over feudalism and capitalism the error has been the illegitimate intrusion of the notion of stage in the very concept of 'mode of production'; in the problem of the specificity of the political instance, it has been the identification of 'production' and 'economy'; in the debates over fascism, it has been the class ascription of elements of ideology; in the case of populism it has been the reductionist equation of 'the people' and classes. The essay 'Feudalism and Capitalism in Latin America' was originally published in *New Left Review,* no 67, 1971, and 'The Specificity of the Political: the Poulantzas-Miliband Debate' in *Economy and Society*, 1975, no 1. The other two essays appear in this volume for the first time. Finally I want to thank those whose useful comments and criticisms have contributed to the final version of the different essays. I must mention, among others, Perry Anderson, Robin Blackburn, Bob Jessop, Harold Wolpe, Sami Zubaida, Enrique Tandeter and Nicos Poulantzas. I am indebted to my students at the University of Essex, with whom these ideas were discussed in numerous courses and seminars, and whose observations and questions frequently enable me to notice ambiguities in my arguments and led me to formulate them more precisely. I would like to thank Elizabeth Nash for her scrupulous labour in rendering my texts from Spanish into English; most of the pages in this book are in debt to her work as translator. And my deepest gratitude must go to Chantal Mouffe, with whom I have discussed exhaustively the major part of these essays. Her contribution to the formulation of some of the central theses has been so decisive that in some respects they may be regarded as a collaborative venture.

1

Feudalism and Capitalism in Latin America

Debate on the Left in the last decade over the origins and present nature of Latin American societies has focused on the problem of whether they should be seen as feudal or capitalist in character. A complex and lengthy discussion has taken place whose importance is not diminished by the conceptual confusion which has often accompanied it. Its significance, moreover, has not been confined to theory, since different theories have led to different political conclusions. Those who maintain that the Latin American societies were historically constituted as feudal in character and have remained so ever since, wish to emphasize that they are closed, traditional, resistant to change and unintegrated into the market economy. If this is the case, then these societies have still not yet reached a capitalist stage and are, indeed, on the eve of a bourgeois-democratic revolution which will stimulate capitalist development and break with feudal stagnation. Socialists should therefore seek an alliance with the national bourgeoisie, and form a united front with it against the oligarchy and imperialism. The advocates of the opposite thesis claim that Latin America has been capitalist from its inception, since it was already fully incorporated into the world market in the colonial period. The present backwardness of Latin American societies is precisely the outcome of the *dependent* character of this incorporation and they are in consequence fully capitalist. It is therefore meaningless to postulate a future stage of capitalist development. It is, on the contrary, necessary to fight directly for socialism, in opposition to a bourgeoisie that is completely integrated with imperialism, forming a common front against the masses.

In this article I hope to contribute to a clarification of the basic terms of the polemic. For despite their contradictory appearance, both the positions first cited coincide in one fundamental respect: both designate by 'capitalism' or 'feudalism' phenomena in the sphere of commodity exchange and not in the sphere of production, thus transforming the presence or absence of a link with the market into the decisive criterion for distinguishing between the two forms of society. Such a conception is clearly alien to Marxist theory, which maintains that feudalism and capitalism are, above all, *modes of production*. André Gunder Frank is one of the best-known defenders of the thesis that Latin America is and always has been capitalist.[2] For this reason the present essay will concentrate on his work since it raises the theoretical issues at stake in the debate in their sharpest and clearest form.

Frank's Theoretical Scheme

Frank's theoretical perspective can be summed up in the following theses:

1. It is false to suppose that economic development occurs through the same succession of stages in each country or that the underdeveloped nations today are at a stage which has been long surpassed by the developed countries. On the contrary, today's developed capitalist countries were never *under*developed in this way, although there was a time when they were *un*developed.

2. It is incorrect to consider contemporary underdevelopment as a simple reflection of the economic, political, cultural and social structures of the underdeveloped country itself. On the contrary, underdevelopment is in large part the historical product of relations between the underdeveloped satellite and the present developed countries. These relations were, moreover, an essential part of the structure and evolution of the capitalist system on a world scale. Thus Frank declares:

[1] This article develops some ideas which I have earlier explored in: 'Feudalism and capitalism as categories of historical analysis' (Internal publication of the Institute Torcuato Di Tella), Buenos Aires, 1968.

[2] *Capitalism and Underdevelopment in Latin America*, New York, 1967, and *Latin America: Underdevelopment or Revolution*, New York, 1969.

'To extract the fruits of their labour through monopoly trade – no less than in the times of Cortez and Pizarro in Mexico and Peru, Clive in India, Rhodes in Africa, the "Open Door" in China – the metropoli destroyed and/or totally transformed the earlier viable social and economic systems of these societies, incorporated them into the metropolitan dominated worldwide capitalist system, and converted them into sources for its own metropolitan capital accumulation and development. The resulting fate for these conquered, transformed or newly acquired established societies was and remains their decapitalization, structurally generated unproductiveness, ever increasing misery for the masses – in a word, their underdevelopment'.[3]

3. The conventional 'dualist' interpretation of Latin American societies must be rejected. The dualist analysis maintains that underdeveloped societies have a dual structure, each one of whose sectors has a dynamic of its own, largely independent of the other. It concludes that the sector which is under the sway of the capitalist world has become modern and relatively developed, while the other sector is confined to an isolated, feudal or pre-capitalist, subsistence economy. According to Frank, this thesis is quite erroneous; the dual structure is wholly illusory, since the expansion of the capitalist system during the last centuries has effectively and completely penetrated even the most apparently isolated sectors of the underdeveloped world.

4. Metropolitan-satellite relations are not limited to the imperial or international level, since they penetrate and structure economic, social and political life in the dependent Latin American countries, creating sub-metropoles within them to which the interior regions are satellites.

5. From the above propositions, Frank derives the following combination of hypotheses: a) In contrast to the world metropolitan centres which are not satellites, the development of the subordinate metropoles is limited by their satellite status; b) the satellites experienced their greatest economic development, including their classical industrial capitalist growth, only when their links with the metropolitan centres were

[3] *Latin America: Underdevelopment or Revolution*, p. 225.

weakened: as was the case during the Spanish Depression of the 17th century, the Napoleonic Wars at the beginning of 19th century, the Depression of the 30's and the two World Wars in the 20th century; by contrast these impulses to development were extinguished whenever the metropolitan centres recovered economically; c) those regions presently most underdeveloped were in the past those most tightly linked to the metropolis; d) the latifundia, whether in the form of plantations or haciendas, were originally typically capitalist commercial enterprises, which themselves created the institutions which enabled them to respond to growing demand in the international and national market, by expanding the aggregate of their capital, land and labour in order to increase their supply of their products; e) latifundia which today are isolated, engaged in subsistence agriculture and apparently semi-feudal, were not always so, but were sectors that underwent a drop in the demand for their output or their productive capacity.

6. Whenever dualism is introduced into a Marxist analysis the implication is that feudalism comprises a conservative sector at one end of the social structure and capitalism a dynamic sector at the other end of it. The strategic consequences are then clear: 'Both in the bourgeois and the supposedly Marxist version of the dual society thesis, one sector of the national economy, which is claimed to have once been feudal, archaic and underdeveloped as well, took off and became the now relatively developed advanced capitalist sector, while the majority of the population stayed in another sector which supposedly remained as it was in its traditionally archaic, feudal, underdeveloped state. The political strategy usually associated with these factually and theoretically erroneous interpretations of development and underdevelopment is for the bourgeois the desirability of extending modernism to the archaic sector and incorporating it into the world and national market as well, and for the Marxists the desirability of completing the capitalist penetration of the feudal countryside and finishing the bourgeois democratic revolution.'[4]

Against this, Frank maintains that Latin America has been

[4] *Op. cit.*, p. 225.

capitalist since its very colonization by European powers in the 16th century. His proof is to show by numerous examples that even the most apparently remote and isolated regions of Latin America participated in the general process of commodity exchange and that this change was to the advantage of the dominant imperialist powers. It would only be appropriate to speak of feudalism, according to Frank, if it could be proved that the most economically backward regions of Latin America constituted a closed universe in which a natural economy predominated. Given that, on the contrary, they participated in a process whose motor force was the thirst for riches of the dominant classes and powers, it is only possible to conclude that we are in the presence of a capitalist economic structure. Since the colonial conquest, capitalism has been the basis of Latin American society and the source of its underdevelopment; it is therefore absurd to propose as an alternative to it a dynamic capitalist development. The national bourgeoisie, in those cases where it exists, is so inextricably linked to the imperialist system and to the exploitative metropolitan/satellite relationship, that policies based on alliance with it can only prolong and accentuate underdevelopment. The national-bourgeois phase in the underdeveloped countries must in consequence be eliminated, or at least abbreviated, rather than extended in the name of the existence of a dual society.

It can be seen that Frank's theoretical schema involves three types of assertion: 1. Latin America has had a market economy from the beginning; 2. Latin America has been capitalist from the beginning; 3. the dependent nature of its insertion into the capitalist world market is the cause of its underdevelopment. The three assertions claim to refer to a single process identical *in its essential aspects* from the 16th to the 20th century. We will analyze in turn each of these aspects.

The Critique of Dualist Conceptions

Frank's criticism of the dualist thesis and his consequent insistence that Latin American societies have always constituted a complex internally structured by, and fully integrated into market economy, are indisputably convincing and correct. Here Frank has developed the cumulative critique of that dualism which received its most celebrated formulation in the work of W. A. Lewis.[5] According to Lewis, who expressed a standpoint to be found in numerous partial studies by social scientists of the previous decade, it was necessary to distinguish carefully between the 'capitalist' sector and the 'subsistence' sector of the economy. The latter was presented as completely stagnant and inferior to the former in capital, income and rate of growth. All relations between the two were reduced to the provision by the backward sector of an unlimited supply of labour to the advanced sector. It has been now repeatedly shown that this model underestimates the degree of commercialization which is possible in rural areas, as well as the degree of accumulation in peasant enterprises. It furthermore greatly over-simplifies and distorts the relations which exist between the two sectors of the economy which it presupposes. A more refined knowledge of the inter-connections between the different sectors of the Latin American economies makes the dualist thesis today no longer tenable in its initial formulation.

Moreover, in the concrete case of Latin America, the evidence accumulated over recent years has completely undermined the idea that a pure, natural economy is to be found in the rural areas of the continent. On the contrary, everything appears to suggest that even the most backward peasant regions are bound by fine threads (which have not yet been adequately studied) to the 'dynamic' sector of the national economy and, through it, to the world market. Alejandro Marroquin in an excellent book[6] has made a regional study of this system of relations. Rodolfo Stavenhagen, analyzing the Maya zone of Chiapas and Guatemala Heights, has shown how inter-ethnic relations serve as the basis for class relations based precisely on a widespread incorporation into the mar-

[5] W. A. Lewis, 'Economic development with Unlimited Supplies of Labour', *Manchester School,* May 1954, pp. 139–91, and idem, *Theory of Economic Growth,* London, 1955. A summary of the criticisms that Lewis's model have aroused can be found in Witold Kula, *An Economic Theory of the Feudal System,* London, NLB, 1976, pp. 21–4. Cf. also P. T. Bauer, 'Lewis's Theory of Economic Growth', *American Economic Review,* XLVI, 1956, 4, pp. 632–41.

[6] Alejandro Marroquin, *La Ciudad Mercado (Tlaxaco),* Mexico, 1957.

ket.[7] Moreover, in Latin America during the colonial period – so often referred to as a phase of closed economy – a wide circulation of commodities prevailed, the axis of which were the mining regions, while the marginal zones were organized as sources of consumption products. In the South of the Continent, for example, the central nucleus was the consumption area of Upper Peru near the Potosi mines, while Chile was transformed into a wheat producer and the Argentinian interior provided manufactured goods for this central nucleus. It is hard to conceive such regional specialization as a pure, natural economy.

The idea of a society with dual structures has a long tradition in Latin America. It was initially formulated in the 19th century by the liberal elites which integrated their countries into the world market as primary producers, thus accommodating them to an international division of labour dictated by the metropolitan imperialist countries. The formula 'civilization or barbarism', coined by Sarmiento, became the watch-word of this process. It was necessary to use every means to discredit the reaction of those interior regions whose relatively diversified economies disintegrated under the impact of competition from European commodities. For this purpose liberal spokesman created a mythology according to which everything colonial was identified with stagnation and all things European with progress: in this Manichean image of the historical dialectic, coexistence between both segments of society became impossible.

This ideological tradition was to prove a heavy impediment to any adequate understanding of the processes which have formed Latin American societies and we cannot say that it has been entirely superseded even today. Much ground has still to be covered by social, economic and anthropological investigation in order to reconstruct the hidden channels of commercialization by which apparently closed economic zones were linked with world markets, and the economic surplus collected from the direct producers. Frank is therefore on solid ground when he criticizes theories of dualism and

[7] Rodolfo Stavenhagen, 'Clases, colonialismos y aculturacíon. Ensayo sobre un sistema de relaciones inter-etnicas en Mesoamerica', *America Latina*, Ano 6, no 4, Outubro–Dezembre 1963, pp. 63–104.

affirms the predominance of the market economy in Latin America. But can we accept his second assertion, that these economies are capitalist?

The Theoretical Mistakes in Frank's Conception

It is not so easy to answer this question since, although his two books are dedicated to the analysis of capitalism, at no time does Frank explain exactly what he means by it. The closest we get to a conceptual characterization in his work is in such expressions as the following:

'Capitalism's essential internal contradiction between the exploiting and the exploited appears within nations no less than between them . . .'[8]

But this does not take us very far, since not only capitalism, but feudalism and indeed every class society has been characterized by the contradiction between exploiters and exploited. The problem is to define in each case the specificity of the exploitative relationship in question. This lack of rigour in determining the object of his analysis is, moreover, only one example of the conceptual imprecision from which all Frank's work suffers; an imprecision that is all the more serious in that Marxists should be well aware of the extensive debates that have occurred over the concept of capitalism,[9] a term which can by no means be taken for granted.

If we nevertheless try to infer what Frank understands by capitalism, I think we can conclude that it is approximately the following: a) a system of production for the market, in which b) profit constitutes the motive of production, and c) this profit is realized for the benefit of someone other than the direct producer, who is thereby dispossessed of it. On the other hand, by feudalism we should understand a closed or subsistence economy. The existence of a substantial market therefore constitutes the decisive difference between the two.

The first surprising thing is that Frank totally dispenses

[8] *Latin America: Underdevelopment or Revolution,* p. 227.

[9] See, for example, Maurice Dobb, *Studies in the Development of Capitalism*, London, 1946, Chapter I and R. H. Hilton, 'Capitalism – What's in a Name?', *Past and Present,* no 1, February 1952, pp. 32–43.

with *relations of production* in his definitions of capitalism and feudalism. In the light of this, his earlier characterization of the relationship between exploiters and exploited as the fundamental contradiction of capitalism ceases to be so puzzling. For, in effect, Frank's ideological perspective obliges him deliberately to omit the relations of production from his definition of capitalism: only by abstracting them can he arrive at a sufficiently wide notion of capitalism to include the different exploitative situations suffered by the indigenous Peruvian peasantry, the Chilean *inquilinos*, the Ecuadorian *huasipungueros*, the slaves of the West Indian sugar plantations or textile workers in Manchester. For all these direct producers assign their produce to the market; they work for the benefit of others, and they are deprived of the economic surplus which they help to create. In all these cases the fundamental economic contradiction is that which opposes the exploiters to the exploited. The only trouble is that the list is too short, for it could also have included the slave on a Roman *latifundium* or the gleb serf of the European Middle Ages, at least in those cases – the overwhelming majority – where the lord assigned part of the economic surplus extracted from the serf for sale. Therefore, we could conclude that from the neolithic revolution onwards there has never been anything but capitalism.

Of course, Frank is at liberty to abstract a mass of historical features and build a model on this basis. He can even, if he wishes, give the resulting entity the name of capitalism, though we cannot see much point in using, to designate such a variety of relations, words which are normally employed in a different sense. But what is wholly unacceptable is the fact that Frank claims that his conception is the Marxist concept of capitalism. *Because for Marx – as is obvious to anyone who has even a superficial acquaintance with his works – capitalism was a mode of production.* The fundamental economic relationship of capitalism is constituted by the free labourer's sale of his labour-power, whose necessary precondition is the loss by the direct producer of ownership of the means of production. In earlier societies the dominant classes exploited the direct producers – that is, expropriated the economic surplus they created – and even commercialized part of this surplus to the extent of permitting the accumulation of large *capitals* by the commercial class. But there was not *capitalism* in the Marxist sense of the term, since no free labour market existed. The following quotation from *Capital* makes this clear:

'. . . otherwise with capital. The historical conditions of its existence are by no means given with the mere circulation of money and commodities. It can spring into life only when the owner of the means of production and subsistence meets in the market with the free labourer selling his labour-power. And this one historical condition comprises a world's history. Capital, therefore, announces from its first appearance a new epoch in the process of social production . . .'[10]

For Marx, the accumulation of commercial capital is perfectly compatible with the most varied modes of production and does not by any means presuppose the existence of a capitalist mode of production:

'. . . Hitherto we have considered merchant's capital merely from the standpoint, and within the limits of, the capitalist mode of production. However, not commerce alone, but also merchant's capital, is older than the capitalist mode of production, is, in fact, historically the oldest free state of existence of capital . . .

'. . . The metamorphosis of commodities, their movement, consists: 1. materially, of the exchange of different commodities for one another, and 2. formally, of the conversion of commodities into money by sale, and of money into commodities by purchase. And the function of merchant's capital resolves itself into these very acts of buying and selling commodities; yet this exchange is not conceived at the outset as a bare exchange of commodities between direct producers. Under slavery, feudalism and vassalage (so far as primitive communities is concerned) it is the slave-owner, the feudal lord, the tribute-collecting state, who are the owners, hence sellers, of the products. The merchant buys and sells for many. Purchases and sales are concentrated in his hands and consequently are no longer bound to the direct requirements of the buyer (as merchant) . . .'[11]

[10] *Capital*, vol. 1. p. 170, Moscow, 1959.
[11] *Op. cit.*, vol. III. pp. 319–21.

Frank's claim that his conception of capitalism is the Marxist one seems to be based on nothing more than his desire for this to be the case. But before leaving this point let us return again to the texts, because, in a polemic that occurred in Mexico and is reflected in his second volume, he was accused *precisely* of ignoring the mode of production in his definition of capitalism. Frank replied with two quotations from Marx which, he claimed, proved his case. The first quotation is taken from the *History of Economic Doctrines* and affirms:

'. . . In the second class of colonies – the plantations, which are from the moment of their inceptions, commercial speculation, centres of production for the world market – a regime of capitalist production exists, if only in a formal way, since slavery among the negroes excludes free wage-labour, which is the base on which capitalist production rests. However, those who deal in slave-trading are capitalists. The system of production introduced by them does not originate in slavery, but was introduced into it. In this case the capitalist and the landlord are one person . . .'

According to Frank, this paragraph proves that for Marx it is not the relations of production that define the nature of an economy (at least I deduce as much since it is his answer to Rodolfo Puiggros's question as to what 'happened inside colonies such as Brazil and those in the Caribbean, that is, where the mode of slave-holding prevailed?'). In reality, the quotation proves exactly the reverse of what Frank intends, since what Marx says is that in the plantation economies the dominant mode of production is only formally capitalist. It is formally capitalist because its beneficiaries participate in a world market in which the dominant productive sectors are already capitalist. This enables the landowners in the plantation economy to participate in the general movement of the capitalist system without, however, their mode of production being capitalist. But what is the essential condition for such a situation is its exceptional character. I think this will be very clear if we compare the paragraph quoted by Frank with another passage by Marx, from *Pre-capitalist Formations*:

'. . . However, this error is certainly no greater than that of, e.g. all philologists who speak of the existence of *capital* in classical antiquity, and of Roman or Greek capitalists. This is merely another way of saying that in Rome and Greece labour was *free*, an assertion which these gentlemen would hardly make. If we talk of plantation owners in America as capitalists, if they *are* capitalists, this is due to the fact that they exist as anomalies within a world market based upon free labour . . .'[12]

Did the structural conditions of capitalism exist in 16th-century Europe when, according to Frank, the process of capitalist domination started in Latin America? Could we consider free labour to be the rule then? By no means. Feudal dependence and urban handicrafts remained the basic forms of productive activity. The existence of a powerful commercial class which greatly enlarged its stock of capital through overseas trade did not in the least modify the decisive fact that this capital was accumulated by the absorption of an economic surplus produced through labour relationships very different from those of free labour. In a classic article, Eric Hobsbawm has located the 17th century as the period of general crisis in the European economy which marked the point of transition towards the capitalist system. As far as the expansion of the 15th and 16th centuries is concerned, however, he affirms on the contrary that:

'. . . Under certain circumstances such trade could, even under feudal conditions, produce a large enough aggregate of profits to give rise to large-scale production; for instance if it catered for exceptionally large organizations such as kingdoms or the church; if the thinly spread demand of an entire continent were concentrated into the hands of businessmen in a few specialized centres such as the Italian and Flemish textile towns; if a large 'lateral extension' of the field of enterprise took place, e.g. by conquest or colonization . . .

'. . . The expansion of the 15th and 16th centuries was essentially, of this sort; and it therefore created its own crisis both within the home market and the overseas market. This crisis the 'feudal businessman' – who were the richest and most powerful just because the best adapted for making big money

[12] Marx, *Pre-capitalist Economic Formations,* London, 1964, pp. 118–19.

in a feudal society – were unable to overcome. Their inadaptability intensified it . . .'[13]

Frank, on the contrary, maintains that European expansion was thoroughly capitalist from the 16th century onwards. He corroborates his assertion with a second quotation from Marx in which the latter declares: 'The modern history of *capitalism* begins with the creation, in the 16th century, of world trade and a world market . . .' But this time Frank happens to have transcribed the quotation badly. In the original, Marx, in fact declares, that: 'The modern history of *capital* dates from the creation in the 16th century of a world-embracing commerce and a world-embracing market . . .'[14]

Given the distinction emphasized above between *capital* and *capitalism* – which permits the coexistence of commercial capital with earlier modes of production – the meaning of this passage is totally different. Marx only says that the enlargement of the world market during the 16th century, brought about by overseas expansion, created the conditions and the global framework in which the *modern* expansion of capital could take place. He takes for granted that anterior forms of capital existed – e.g. in the Middle Ages or in Antiquity. But he by no means speaks of capitalism.

The errors of Frank's conception can be seen from the fact that he has defined capitalism so loosely that he is unable legitimately to derive any concrete consequences from it about anything. This is, of course, not his own belief: he is confident that he can demonstrate on this ground the irrelevance of the bourgeois-democratic stage in Latin America. Let us consider this demonstration. Frank's basic assertion is that since the task of the bourgeois-democratic revolution is to destroy feudalism, whereas capitalism has always existed in Latin America *ab initio*, the bourgeois democratic revolution disappears from the revolutionary calendar, and is replaced by a direct struggle for socialism.

But Frank has again confused the terms of the problem. For when Marxists speak of a democratic revolution sweeping

[13] E. J. Hobsbawm, 'The Crisis of the 17th Century', *Past and Present*, no 5, May 1954, p. 41.
[14] Marx, *Capital*, vol. 1, ed. cit., p. 146.

away the vestiges of feudalism, they understand by feudalism something very different from Frank. For them feudalism does not mean a closed system which market forces have not penetrated, but a general ensemble of extra-economic coercions weighing on the peasantry, absorbing a good part of its economic surplus, and thereby retarding the process of internal differentiation within the rural classes, and therefore the expansion of agrarian capitalism. This is also what the French revolutionaries of 1789 understood by feudalism when they thought they were suppressing it by abolishing the *gabelles* and seigneurial privileges. When Lenin speaks of the growing weight of capitalism in the agrarian structure of Russia in *The Development of Capitalism in Russia*, his aim is to demonstrate a growing process of class differentiation which was gradually producing a class of rich peasants, on the one hand, and an agricultural proletariat, on the other. It would not have occurred to Lenin to base his demonstration of this process on a progressive expansion of production for the market, for such production had *precisely* formed the source of feudalism in Russia several centuries before, when growing opportunities for commercialized wheat production had led the landowners to increase – indeed to establish – the oppression of serfdom. When the Bolsheviks maintained that the tasks of the Russian Revolution were bourgeois-democratic, they meant that it would eliminate the vestiges of feudalism and open the door to capitalist expansion (in 1905 only Trotsky and Parvus grasped that Russian conditions made possible the inauguration of the direct transition to socialism). Given the inability of the bourgeoisie to carry through its democratic tasks and the numerical weakness of the proletariat, they imagined that the peasantry would have to play a decisive role in the alliance which seized power. For such a strategy, it was crucial that the peasant problem could not be solved by the existing régime, since otherwise Tsarism could have built its own road to capitalism and the revolution would have been postponed *sine die*. Stolypin, the Tsarist Minister who used every device to promote the emergence of a strong class of peasant proprietors to become a bulwark of reaction – somewhat similar to the French peasantry from Napoleon I to de Gaulle – understood this as well as the Bolsheviks. The danger of his policy was clearly perceived by Lenin when he wrote in 1908:

'. . . The Stolypin Constitution and the Stolypin agrarian policy mark a new phase in the breakdown of the old, semi-patriarchal and semi-feudal system of Tsarism, a new movement towards its transformation into a middle-class monarchy . . . If this should continue for very long periods of time . . . it might force us to renounce any agrarian programme at all. It would be empty and stupid democratic phrase-mongering to say that the success of such a policy in Russia is 'impossible'. It is possible! If the Stolypin policy is continued . . . then the agrarian structure of Russia will become completely bourgeois, the stronger peasants will acquire almost all the allotments of land, agriculture become capitalistic, and any 'solution' of the agrarian problem – radical or otherwise – will become impossible under capitalism . . .'

This passage limpidly illustrates the conditions in which Lenin considered capitalist development could remove the bourgeois-democratic stage from the agenda of the revolution – exactly the problem with which Frank is grappling. These conditions were the emergence of a strong kulak class at one extreme, and the growth of a rural proletariat on the other. Frank's denial of the possibility of a bourgeois-democratic revolution in Latin America in effect only amounts to this: he takes a political schema based on an analysis of social relationships respectively designated feudalism and capitalism, he modifies the content of these concepts in mid-stream and then concludes that the political schema is false because it does not correspond to reality. There is no need to insist on the validity of this type of reasoning. (Let me add that I am in no way concerned here to assess the possibility or impossibility of a bourgeois-democratic stage in the various countries of Latin America. I have limited myself to pointing out the impossibility of formulating any prognosis on this question on the basis of Frank's analysis.)

Furthermore, if we took Frank's definitions of capitalism and feudalism literally, we would have to derive much more from them than Frank claims. In fact if capitalism had already become general in the metropolitan countries by the 16th century – and it is not clear why he stops there when trade and a market economy prevailed from much earlier times – we would have to conclude that Elizabethan England or Renaissance France were ripe for socialism, something I do not think even Frank himself would be prepared to suggest.

If we now confront Frank's affirmation that the socio-economic complexes of Latin America have been capitalist since the Conquest Period (bearing in mind that capitalism and feudalism are modes of production in the Marxist sense of the term) with the currently available empirical evidence, we must conclude that the 'capitalist' thesis is indefensible. In regions with dense indigenous populations – Mexico, Peru, Bolivia, or Guatemala – the direct producers were not despoiled of their ownership of the means of production, while extra-economic coercion to maximize various systems of labour service – in which it is impossible not to see the equivalent of the European *corvée* – was progressively intensified. In the plantations of the West Indies, the economy was based on a mode of production constituted by slave labour, while in the mining areas there developed disguised forms of slavery and other types of forced labour which bore not the slightest resemblance to the formation of a capitalist proletariat. Only in the pampas of Argentina in Uruguay, and in other similar small areas where no indigenous population had previously existed – or where it had been very scarce and was rapidly wiped out – did settlement assume capitalist forms from the beginning, which were then accentuated by the massive immigration of the 19th century. But these regions were very remote from the dominant pattern in Latin America, and were more akin to the new settlements in temperate zones like Australia and New Zealand.

Now this pre-capitalist character of the dominant relations of production in Latin America was not only *not* incompatible with production for the world market, but was actually intensified by the expansion of the latter. The feudal regime of the haciendas tended to increase its servile exactions on the peasantry as the growing demands of the world market stimulated maximization of their surplus. Thus, far from expansion of the external market acting as a disintegrating force on feudalism, its effect was rather to accentuate and consolidate it. Let us take an example from Frank's analysis: the evolution of *in-*

quilinaje (a form of leasehold) in Chile. During the 17th century, the tenant obtained lease of his lands in lieu of a symbolic payment, but this payment began to acquire economic significance and to weigh ever more heavily on the peasant holding as wheat exports to Peru developed following the earthquake of 1688. The 19th century witnessed an aggravation of this process, determined yet again by the increased cereal exports; the labour exacted was often equivalent to that of a permanent worker while the traditional rights of the peasant were simultaneously reduced, especially his right to *talaje* or pasturage. The money wage he now obtained was lower than that of a day labourer or a journeyman. It would be a mistake to see in this process the emergence of a rural proletariat. If this had been the case the wage should have become the major part of the *inquilinos*' means of subsistence. But all the signs show that, on the contrary, the wage was merely one subordinate element in a subsistence economy based on land tenancy. That is to say, we are faced with a peasant subjected to servile obligations and not with an agricultural wage-earner who completes his income with customary privileges and a piece of land. [15]

[15] In an unpublished note that the author has kindly made available to me, Juan Martinez Alier has pointed out that on the haciendas of the Peruvian Sierra, where the formal elements of extra-economic coercion – such as *corvée* in economic and *gamonalismo* in political relations – have not disappeared, they have nevertheless been transformed to the extent that the peasants' land hunger is now an instrumental end and not an end in itself: land hunger now stems in reality from hunger for employment. He adds: 'The aim of a classical jacquerie is to throw off the boss: that is to say, to recover full possession of the land, to get rid of the obligation to pay rent, and as a result, to change the political structure of the distribution of power. The aims of a struggle by peasants with a proletarian mentality will be, on the other hand, to obtain higher pay and greater security, and for those goals the acquisition of land or its take-over by the State can seem appropriate means. If we think . . . that, for the non-wage earning peasant of the Sierra who has gone to work in the haciendas, the principal problem is security of employment, then the possibilities of locating an agrarian structure which permits later socialist development are greater than if we think that the possession of the land is an end in itself for the peasants.'

Martinez Alier here points out one of the ways in which a process of proletarianization can effectively start. Nevertheless, the operation of this process presupposes the concurrence of two conditions: 1) that there is a progressive loss of ownership of the means of production; 2) that another optional system of employment, subject to cyclical fluctuations, is permanently available. Otherwise we should have to maintain that where the demand for service labour is lower than the supply, coercion is economic and not extra-economic,

This situation – with some variations – was repeated monotonously throughout the Continent. Thus Latin America was not an exception to the process by which heavily settled marginal regions experienced a strengthening of servile relations to increase production for external markets. This is what Eastern Europe progressively experienced from the 16th century onwards, when a substantial growth in the export of primary products to the West became possible. This process was the basis for the re-feudalization of peripheral areas, the 'second servitude' of which Engels speaks. No doubt from the end of the 19th century these conditions were gradually modified in Latin America with the progressive growth of a rural proletariat. It is difficult to say how far peasant proletarianization has reached in different areas today, since we lack sufficient studies of it, but there is no doubt that the process is very far from being concluded, and semi-feudal conditions are still widely characteristic of the Latin American countryside. There is no need whatever to draw dualist perspectives from this position, because we have already seen that the basis of the modern, expanding sector was provided by increased servile exploitation in the backward sector.

We now reach the point where the fundamental misunderstanding in this polemic rests; *to affirm the feudal character of relations of production in the agrarian sector does not necessarily involve maintaining a dualist thesis.* Dualism implies that no connections exist between the 'modern' or 'progressive' sector and the 'closed' or 'traditional' sector. Yet we have argued that, on the contrary, servile exploitation was accentuated and consolidated by the very tendency of entrepreneurs – presumably 'modern' in type – to maximize profits; the apparent lack of communication between the two sectors herewith

---

and that therefore the serf is a proletarian and not a peasant. But this situation was a frequent occurrence during the European Middle Ages in periods of rising population, which enabled the lords to intensify the services due to them. On the other hand, periods of declining population – such as that which followed the Black Death in the 14th century – enabled the peasants to improve their negotiating position vis à vis the lord. The situation described by Martinez Alier only exists when land has become simply one possible field of employment alongside others. In all other cases, we cannot speak of a dissociation in the peasant's consciousness between the land as a source of employment and the land as an end in itself.

disappears. In such cases we can affirm that the modernity of one sector is a function of the backwardness of the other, and that therefore no policy is revolutionary which poses as the 'left-wing' of the 'modernizing sector'. It is, on the contrary, correct to confront the system as a whole and to show the indissoluble unity that exists between the maintenance of feudal backwardness at one extreme and the apparent progress of a bourgeois dynamism at the other. I believe that in this way we can effectively demonstrate, in agreement with Frank, that development does generate underdevelopment, except that we base our reasoning on relations of production and not only on those of the market. Frank can, nevertheless, argue that the defenders of the 'feudal' thesis – notoriously the Latin American Communist Parties – have upheld dualist positions. There is undoubtedly much truth in this. For in their interpretation of the nature of the Latin American economies, the 'feudalists' have employed definitions of feudalism and capitalism similar to Frank's own. It would take too long to explain the reasons for this deformation now, but I believe they can be summed up in this fact: historically, the Latin American left emerged as the left wing of liberalism and its ideology was correspondingly determined by the basic categories of the liberal élites of the 19th century, which we have already outlined. Dualism was an essential element in this system of categories. From this source there derived a constant tendency to identify feudalism with stagnation and closed economy, and capitalism with dynamism and progress. This typical deformation of Marxism then generated its dialectical complement in the diametrically opposite position, that has emerged during the last decade. Since knowledge of historical and present reality made it increasingly evident that the Latin American economies had *always* been market economies, and since the political failure of reformist and allegedly progressive elites in Latin America revealed ever more clearly the intimate interconnections between 'modern' and 'traditional' sectors, a new school concluded that Latin America had always been capitalist. Frank and those who think like him – and there are many – accept the terms of the dilemma as the Latin American CPs and 19th-century liberals have posed them, but they place themselves at the opposite extreme. They thus undoubtedly break with dualism – and their point of view is therefore relatively more correct – *but by trying to situate the fundamental contradiction in the field of circulation rather than production they can go no more than half-way towards an explanation of why development generates underdevelopment.* This becomes very clear once we move on to analyze Frank's third type of assertion, to which we have previously referred: those according to which the origins of underdevelopment lie in the dependent character of Latin American economic insertion into the world market. But before dealing with this point, it is necessary to introduce a greater degree of precision into the analytic categories we will use by distinguishing in particular between modes of production and economic systems.

Modes of Production and Economic Systems[16]

We understand by 'mode of production' an integrated complex of social productive forces and relations linked to a determinate type of ownership of the means of production.[17] From among the ensemble of relations of production, we consider those linked to the ownership of the means of production to be the essential relations, since they determine the forms of canalization of the economic surplus and the effective degree of the division of labour, the basis in turn of the specific capacity of the productive forces for expansion. Their own level and rhythm of growth depends in turn on the destination of the economic surplus. We therefore designate as a mode of production the logical and mutually co-ordinated articulation of: 1. a determinate type of ownership of the means of production; 2. a determinate form of appropriation of the economic surplus; 3. a determinate degree of development of the division of labour; 4. a determinate level of development of the productive forces. This is not merely a descriptive enumeration of isolated 'factors', but a totality defined by its mutual interconnections. Within this totality, property in the means of production constitutes the decisive element.

An 'economic system', on the other hand, designates the

[16] What follows is a resumé of arguments advanced in my study mentioned above (see footnote 1).
[17] Oscar Lange, *Economia Politica*, Roma, 1962.

mutual relations between the different sectors of the economy, or between different productive units, whether on a regional, national or world scale. When, in Volume One of *Capital*, Marx analyzed the process of production of surplus value and the accumulation of capital, he described the *capitalist mode of production*. On the other hand, when he analyzes the interchange between Department One and Department Two and introduces problems such as rent or the origin of commercial profit, he is describing an 'economic system'. An economic system can include, as constitutive elements, different modes of production – provided always that we define it as a whole, that is, by proceeding from the element or law of motion that establishes the unity of its different manifestations.

The feudal mode of production is one in which the productive process operates according to the following pattern: 1. the economic surplus is produced, by a labour force subject to economic compulsion; 2. the economic surplus is privately appropriated by someone other than the direct producer; 3. property in the means of production remains in the hands of the direct producer. In the capitalist mode of production, the economic surplus is also subject to private appropriation, but as distinct from feudalism, ownership of the means of production is severed from ownership of labour-power; it is that which permits the transformation of labour-power into a commodity, and with this the birth of the wage-relation. I believe it is possible within this theoretical framework to situate the problem of dependence at the level of relations of production.

The Stages of Dependence

Frank refers throughout his works to the relation of dependence between satellite and metropolis; indeed this is the axis along which his theoretical schema is organized. Nevertheless, throughout his writings there is no attempt whatever to define the nature of this relationship of dependence – that is, to situate the specific economic contradictions on which the relationship of dependence hinges. Frank describes for us a situation in which the underdeveloped country is totally integrated into the expansive processes of the great metropolitan countries; he then shows us *how* the advanced countries have exploited the peripheral countries; what he at no time explains is *why* certain nations needed the underdevelopment of other nations for their own process of expansion. The most he provides on this point is a vague general reference to Paul Baran's *The Political Economy of Growth.* But as we know, Baran deals with a very specific situation of underdevelopment, which we cannot extrapolate into the past and which is becoming constantly less applicable today to contemporary Latin America. Or does Frank believe that Baran's model is applicable to such countries as Argentina, Brazil or Mexico – the three most important areas of investment in the continent, after Venezuela, for North American imperialism?

It is not very difficult to find the reasons for this notable gap in Frank's theoretical schema. For his notion of capitalism is so wide that, given the level of abstraction on which he moves, he cannot define any contradictions that are specific to it. If Cortes, Pizarro, Clive and Cecil Rhodes are all one and the same, there is no way of tracing the nature and origins of economic dependence in relation of production. If, on the other hand, we cease to regard capitalism as a *Deus ex Machina* whose omnipresence frees us from all explanatory problems, and try instead to trace the origins of dependence in concrete modes to production, the first step we must take is to renounce all talk of a single unique contradiction. Because relationships of dependence have always existed on the margins of the existence of capitalism.

During the Middle Ages, for example, advances in historiographic studies have made it clear that an unequal exchange existed between Western Europe and the Eastern Mediterranean. Ashtor's works on prices in medieval Syria, in particular, show that the latter were stationary while prices in Western Europe were oscillating with a long-term tendency to rise. This disjuncture provided a channel of absorption of economic surplus for the Western bourgeoisies from their Eastern periphery. Since economic dependence means the constant absorption by one region of the economic surplus of another region, we must categorize medieval trade between East and West as a relation of dependence, because the disparity in price levels – the basis of any commercial activity – was always to the advantage of one against the other. Yet this activity, which greatly stimulated the accumulation of commercial capital in the great European cities, by no means implied the generalization of wage relationships in the sphere of production. On the contrary, it corresponded to a feudal expansion, in which servile ties were very often reinforced to maximize the surplus. Was not the European expansion of the mercantilist epoch perhaps an extension of this process on a world scale? Through its monopoly positions, metropolitan Europe fixed the price of commodities in its overseas empires – with the aim of securing a permanent disparity in its favour – while, by means of extra-economic coercion, it exploited labour-power in the mines and plantation systems. Romano asks: 'Can the problem of disparity of prices, observed between different regions of the Near East, find an explanation, an attempted explanation, in the light of the example of Spanish America? Might not these zones of lower price levels be the fate of sub-colonies, such as are so often found in the Spanish Empire in America: for example, Chile and Peru were both colonies of Spain, yet the first was also the sub-colony of the second? . . .'[18] It is thus possible to see how the development of the dominant economic structure of the metropolitan countries in the mercantilist epoch could generate underdevelopment: reducing the economic surplus of the peripheral countries and fixing their relations of production in an archaic mould of extra-economic coercion, which retarded any process of social differentiation and diminished the size of their internal markets.

This type of dependent relationship is nevertheless very different from that which was to predominate in the specifically capitalist epoch of European expansion. For this is where the central problem arises. Because if we want to show that in this epoch too, development generates underdevelopment, what we have to prove is that the maintenance of pre-capitalist relations of production in the peripheral areas is an inherent condition of the process of accumulation in the central countries. At this point we enter territory where unfortunately empirical investigation is too inadequate to permit our reaching any

[18] Ruggiero Romano, 'Les prix au Moyen Age: dans le Proche Orient et dans l'Occident chrétien', *Annales E.S.C.*, juillet-août 1963, pp. 699–702.

definitive conclusion;[19] nevertheless I believe we can legitimately formulate a theoretical model which establishes the variables at play and the form of their articulation to which the available evidence points. This theoretical model can be summarized in the following terms. The process of capital accumulation – which is the fundamental motor force of the ensemble of the capitalist system – depends on the rate of profit. Now the rate of profit is in its turn determined by the rate of surplus-value and the organic composition of capital. A rise in the organic composition of capital is a condition for capitalist expansion, since technological progress is what permits the reconstitution of the reserve army of labour and the maintenance of a low level of wages. But unless a rise in the organic composition of capital is linked to a more than proportional increase in the rate of surplus value, it will necessarily produce a decline in the rate of profit. This tendency is partially compensated by capital movements from industries with a high organic composition to those with a low organic composition: from this there emerges an average rate of profit which is always higher in value terms than the corresponding rate of profit in the technologically more advanced industries. Nevertheless, since a growing augmentation in the organic composition of the total capital is inherent in capitalist expansion, in the long term there can only be a permanent tendency for the rate of profit to decline. These are, of course, the terms of the famous law formulated by Marx.

It will be seen that in this schema – which describes precisely enough the dominant tendencies at work in a free competitive capitalism – what seems to be the key to a sustained process of accumulation is the expansion, in any sector of the system, of productive units in which either low technology or super-exploitation of labour makes it possible to counteract the depressive effect on the rate of profit of the increasing organic composition of capital in the dynamic or advanced industries. Now the enterprises of the peripheral areas are in an ideal position to play this role. Let us take the example of plantations

[19] See, however, the information contained in the essays by Cristian Palloix, 'Impérialisme et mode de production capitaliste' in *L'Homme et la Société*, no 12, avril-juin 1969, pp. 175–94, and Samir Amin, 'Le commerce international et le flux internationaux de capitaux', *ibid.*, no 15, janvier-mars 1970, pp. 77–102.

or haciendas. In these the organic composition of capital is low[20] – as is always the case in the production of primary products as against industrial output; the labour force is in general subjected to the forms of extra-economic coercion characteristic of the feudal or slave modes of production; finally, to the extent that free labour exists, it is generally superabundant and therefore cheap.[21] If it could then be proved that investment in these sectors has played an important role in determining the rate of profit, it would follow that the expansion of industrial capitalism in the metropolitan countries necessarily depended on the maintenance of pre-capitalist modes of production in the peripheral areas. However it is at this point that the evidence so far available becomes suggestive, but not conclusive. If this thesis were established it would be possible by starting strictly from relations of production, to show that development generates underdevelopment and to refute, from a Marxist perspective, the traditional

[20] Under feudalism the ownership of the means of production by the direct producer is an obstacle to technical progress. Under a slave mode of production the tendency of the slave to destroy the machine creates barriers to investment of constant capital. See Marx, *Capital*, vol. I, pp. 196–7, where several examples are cited, and Manuel Moreno Fraginals, *El Ingenio,* La Habana, 1964.

[21] The importance of this fact was already noted by Marx, who nevertheless did not analyze its relative weight in the formation of average rate of profit: 'Another question – really beyond the scope of our analysis because of its special nature – is this: Is the general rate of profit raised by the higher rate of profit produced by capital invested in foreign, and particularly colonial, trade?

Capital invested in foreign trade can yield a higher rate of profit, because, in the first place, there is competition with commodities produced in other countries with inferior production facilities, so that the more advanced country sells its goods cheaper than the competing countries. In so far as the labour of the more advanced country is here realized as labour of a higher specific weight, the rate of profit rises, because labour which has not been paid as being of a higher quality is sold as such. The same may obtain in relation to the country to which commodities are exported and to that from which commodities are imported: namely, the latter may offer more materialized labour *in kind* than it receives and yet thereby receive commodities cheaper than it could produce them. Just as a manufacturer who employs a new invention before it becomes generally used, undersells his competitors and yet sells his commodity above its individual value, that is, realizes the specifically higher productiveness of the labour he employs as surplus labour. He thus secures a surplus profit. As concerns capital invested in colonies, etc., on the other hand, they may yield higher rates of profit for the simple reason that the rate of profit is higher there due to backward development, and likewise the exploitation of labour, because of the use of slaves, coolies, etc'. *Capital,* vol. III, pp. 232–3.

dualist schema.

Returning, then, to our previous terminology, we can affirm that the world capitalist system – which finds its regulating principle in the average rate of profit produced by the interaction between different enterprises – includes, *at the level of its definition,* various modes of production For if our previous line of argument is correct, the growth of the system depends on the accumulation of capital, the rhythm of this accumulation depends on the average rate of profit, and the level of this rate depends in its turn on the consolidation and expansion of pre-capitalist relationships in the peripheral areas. The great flaw in pure underconsumptionist theories is that they interpret external expansion as a response to the pressure for markets; they thereby overlook the decisive fact that colonial exploitation, by helping to raise the average rate of profit, ensures the system's capacity for expansion not only at the moment of *realization* but also at the moment of *investment.*

This is as far as we can go by purely theoretical argument. The above assertions are subject to two series of empirical verifications. It will be necessary to demonstrate: 1) that during the 19th century the growth in the organic composition of capital was in fact more rapid than the growth in the productivity of labour; 2) that the capital invested in peripheral countries played an important role in the maintenance of an adequate rate of profit in the metropolitan countries. Only empirical investigation can prove that both these conditions existed in reality.

On the other hand, if these conditions did exist in the past, there is no doubt that they no longer apply today.[22] The enormous increase in the productivity of labour in the present stage of monopoly capitalism – related to technological changes – has tended to make pre-capitalist super-exploitation of labour power anti-economic, and to concentrate investment in the central countries. At the same time – Latin America is a clear example of this – imperialist investment has tended to shift from its traditional patterns into the production of either

[22] See for example, the discussion initiated by Charles Bettelheim in his preface to the French edition of Baran and Sweezy's *Monopoly Capital* (Paris, 1968) and by Pierre Jalée, *L'Imperialisme en 1970* (Paris, 1970).

strategic materials – the typical case is oil – or into industrial output. The nature of the relationship between metropolis and satellite – to use Frank's terminology – is no less one of dependence, but it operates in each case as a very distinct type of dependence. It seems to me more useful to underline these differences and discontinuities than to attempt to show the continuity and identity of the process, from Hernan Cortes to General Motors.

Returning, then, to the debate over 'feudalism vs. capitalism', I think it should by now be clear that its protagonists have constantly confused the two concepts of the *capitalist mode of production* and *participation in a world capitalist economic system.* I consider that the distinction between these concepts is not a purely academic matter since, if the foregoing argument is correct, it enables us to clarify important aspects of the ensemble of relationships between metropolis and satellite. On the other hand, to equate the two can only perpetuate the misunderstanding that haunts Frank's contribution to the debate. The final comment on the traditional form of the polemic can perhaps best be left to Marx himself. In a celebrated reflection on the economists of his day he wrote a passage that has still not lost its relevance:

'The first theoretical treatment of the modern mode of production – the mercantile system – proceeded necessarily from the superficial phenomena of the circulation process as individualized in the movements of merchant capital, and therefore grasped only the appearance of matters. Partly because merchant's capital is the first free state of existence of capital in general. And partly because of the overwhelming influence which it exerted during the first revolutionizing period of feudal production – the genesis of modern production. The real science of modern economy only begins when the theoretical analysis passes from the process of circulation to the process of production . . . .'[23]

[23] *Capital*, vol. III, p. 331.

Postscript

This essay was originally published six years ago, and gained some considerable influence. It was widely commented upon both in England and in Latin America, and gave rise to some important debates. It is included in this volume – despite the fact that the notion of mode of production which it employs now seems to me inadequate – because I think that its basic thesis remains correct and because circulationist positions, although in retreat, continue to be an important source of errors within Marxist theory. In this brief postscript I would like to present the following thesis: that Marxist thought in Latin America has found considerable difficulty in moving *simultaneously* at the level of *modes of production* and at that of *economic systems,* and that its most frequent mistakes derive from a unilateral use of one or other of the two levels.

My essay had a dual intention. 1) It sought to try and separate *the concept* of mode of production from any historical connotation, that is to say, from any link with a necessary stage of development. 'Mode of production' is an abstract concept and not a stage of concrete historical development. There is, therefore, no historical transformation that can be explained *exclusively* by unfolding the internal logic of a determinate mode of production. 2) It sought to conceive concrete economies as systems of relations constituted by the articulation of different modes of production. Hence I put forward the distinction between 'modes of production' and 'economic systems', which I continue to think correct and necessary. Any advance towards the concrete involves a progressive analytical transition from modes of production to economic systems. Obviously this still remains an abstract analysis; the final step to the concrete would need the economic system to be situated in relation to the political and ideological levels which characterize any determinate social formation. In any case, remaining on the strictly economic plane, it is clear that the more concrete the analysis, the broader and more complex will be the system of relations to be analyzed. It is obvious that the dimensions of this system, conceived as a totality, have tended to be identified from the 16th century onwards with the world market. To what extent was this world economic system capitalist? As we have argued, the world economic system is capitalist to the extent that the law of motion of the capitalist mode of production – that is to say, the fluctuations in the rate of profit (which is a strictly capitalist category, $\frac{s}{c+v}$, since it presupposes the existence of free labour) – has come to be the law of motion which articulates the system as a whole. It is this that permits the coexistence of various non-capitalist modes of production to be articulated within the world capitalist system.[1] As we have argued, the structural changes which the capitalist mode of production has experienced in metropolitan countries can in many cases contribute to a strengthening of extra-economic exploitation of labour in peripheral areas. The concept of 'world capitalist system' is therefore the nearest approximation to the concrete which a merely economic analysis permits, and if what we have asserted in this essay is correct, it cannot be *derived* from the concept of 'capitalist mode of production' but must be *constructed* by starting from a theoretical study of possible articulations of the different modes of production. The analysis of these is thus a precondition of a *theoretical* study of the world capitalist system. Any different course cannot proceed beyond the empirico-descriptive stage.

A good example of the theoretical errors to which an ingenuous empiricism leads in social sciences can be found in the

[1] Note that it is not possible to evade the problem by saying that profit is not a capitalist category, since it is present in any society where an economic surplus passes into hands other than those of the direct producer. If we define the concept of 'profit' in these terms, we are referring to a concept different from 'capitalist profit'. The specific laws governing the movement of the latter depend on a complex of relations – rate of profit, organic composition of capital, etc. – which only arise in so far as labour power has come to be a commodity, that is to say, with capitalism. The condition for speaking of the *world capitalist system* is not, therefore, that the system be unified by the tendency of a *homo economicus* to maximize his interests, outside any specific type of production relations, but that the laws of motion of the rate of profit, *conceived as a capitalist category*, determine the laws of motion of the whole system. To formulate the problem thus conforms with the arguments of my essay – that is to say, the need to see the world capitalist system as an articulation of numerous economic units which produce on the basis of various modes of production, and whose unity is provided by the movements of the rate of profit. We are concerned with the movements of the latter conceived as a general category, determined by changes in that sector of the system in which the capitalist mode of production predominates.

now well-known work of Immanuel Wallerstein.[2] This author has tried to pose the very problem we have been discussing: his aim has been to understand the capitalist *system* as a totality whose dimensions coincide with the world market and which is incomprehensible if we analyze its isolated parts. However, he has tried to do so by following a different course: by reducing the concept of 'mode of production' to that of 'economic system'. He states, in a critical analysis of my position: 'Western Europe, at least England from the late seventeenth century on, had primarily landless, wage-earning labourers. In Latin America, then and to some extent still now, labourers were not proletarians but slaves or "serfs". If proletariat then capitalism. Of course. To be sure. But is England, or Mexico, or the West Indies a unit of analysis? Does each have a separate "mode of production"? Or is the unit (for the sixteenth–eighteenth centuries) the European world-economy, including England *and* Mexico, in which case what was the mode of production of this world economy? . . .'[3]

That is to say, by mode of production we no longer understand the relation between productive forces and relations of production but international economic relations, since the mode of production is identified with the world economy as such. Wallerstein started from the correct observation that it is not possible to link the dominant mode of production in a country or a region with a determinate stage of development, since the intelligibility of any process of change depends on an analysis of the world economy as a whole and not of its isolated parts; but instead of concluding that by mode of production we should therefore understand an analytical category devoid of 'stageist' connotations, he has transferred the stages to the economic system and has eliminated – by a distortion – the concept of mode of production. Consequently, the world capitalist economic system is not *the result* of a theoretical construction but the *starting point* of analysis. Wallerstein claims that his analysis

[2] I. Wallerstein, *The Modern World System: Capitalist Agriculture and the Origins of European World Economy in the Sixteenth Century*, New York, 1974; 'The Rise and Future Demise of the World Capitalist System: Concepts for Comparative Analysis', *Comparative Studies in Society and History*, vol. 16, no 4, 1974.

[3] I. Wallerstein, 'The Rise and Future . . .', p. 394.

is based on the primacy of the category of totality. But his is not a rich and complex totality of theoretical determinations, resulting from a progressive process of approximation to the concrete, but exactly the opposite: it is a vacant and homogeneous totality created by eliminating differences instead of articulating them. Thus, he states, for example: 'This, then resolves the problem incurred by using the pervasiveness of wage-labour as a defining characteristic of capitalism. An individual is no less a capitalist exploiting labour because the state assists him to pay his labourers low wages (including wages in kind) and denies these labourers the right to change employment. Slavery and so-called "second serfdom" are not to be regarded as anomalies in a capitalist system . . . This is a relationship in which labour-power is a commodity (how could it ever be more so than under slavery?), quite different from the relationship of a feudal serf to his lord in eleventh century Burgundy, where the economy was not oriented to a world market, and where labour-power was in no sense bought or sold. Capitalism thus means labour as a commodity to be sure. But in the era of agricultural capitalism, wage-labour is only one of the modes in which labour is recruited and recompensed in the labour market. Slavery, coerced cash crop production (my name for the so-called "second feudalism"), share-cropping and tenancy are all alternative modes'.[4]

We may pass over various errors in this paragraph, some of which are familiar – such as the confusion between labour and labour-power or the assertion that labour-power is a commodity under slavery – while others are quizzical – slavery as a recompense for labour! Rather let us concentrate on the results of this process of theoretical homogenization to which the most varied of modes of production are subjected. Fulfilling our worst expectations, the most concrete of economic systems – the world capitalist system – has come to be the most abstract: its unifying principle is constituted by the search for profit in the market by capitalists and the resulting division of labour. Speaking of European agriculture in the sixteenth century, Wallerstein says: 'If capitalism is a mode of production, production for profit in a market, then we ought, I should have

[4] *Op. cit.*, p. 400.

thought, to look to whether or not such production was or was not occurring. It turns out in fact that it was, and in a very substantial form . . .'[5] The conclusion is hardly surprising. If the only defining feature of the capitalist mode of production is constituted by the individual motivations of its agents – the seeking of profit in the market – we will find capitalism throughout history. The system is thus unified by a merely subjective principle, while relations of production are reduced to the role of mere technical accidents dictated by world conditions and factors of production. The result has nothing in common with the complexity of the concrete that is characteristic of the Marxist totality; rather it recalls the elimination of social relations characteristic of neoclassical economics, with its exclusive emphasis on the market.[6] It is not surprising then, that Wallerstein's endeavour culminates in a merely factual and erudite survey, without the slightest indication of theoretical explanation.

[5] *Op. cit.*, p. 399.

[6] I doubt, however, whether Wallerstein would be convinced by this argument, since he accuses me on many occasions of being faithful to the letter of Marx but not to his spirit. Let us see, however, the result of Wallerstein's spiritual undertaking: 'Laclau precisely beclouds the issue . . . The point is that the "relations of production" that define a system are the "relations of production" of the whole system, and the system at this point in time is the European world-economy. Free labour is indeed a defining feature of capitalism, but not free labour throughout the productive enterprises. Free labour is the form of labour control used for skilled work in core countries whereas coerced labour is used for less skilled work in peripheral areas. The combination thereof is the essence of capitalism. When labour is everywhere free we shall have socialism . . .' (*The Modern World System*, pp. 126–7). I confess I had to read this paragraph three times to convince myself that I had not misunderstood it. But there is no possible room for doubt: Wallerstein does not appear to be aware of the meaning of 'free labour'. Any Marxist knows that under capitalism labour power is *free* because it is not subjected to any extra-economic coercion, and that it is *freely* sold on the market because the worker has been deprived of property in the means of production. This is the basis of the wage relation, which constitutes the essence of capitalism and whose abolition is precisely constituted by socialism. Wallerstein, on the contrary, develops the bizarre idea that socialism consists in the generalization of wage relations throughout the planet. This is not, perhaps, so surprising when we note that in the same paragraph Wallerstein reduces extra-economic coercion – which it is well-known constitutes the basis of productive relations in non-capitalist modes of production – to a mere technical means of organizing unskilled work. Examples like these make me think that Wallerstein has confused the spirit of Marx with the evil genius of Descartes, that took delight in deceiving him.

If we compare the method of approximating to the concrete characteristic of *Capital*, we observe a very different process. Marx begins with the most abstract of relations and hence analyzes the commodity and exchange in general. He then analyzes in what sense these relations are modified when labour-power is transformed into a commodity – from here there proceeds the whole analysis of surplus-value and the accumulation process. Then in Volume II the study shifts from the capitalist mode of production to the capitalist economic system with an analysis of the exchange between Department I and Department II. Later on categories such as rent and commercial profit are introduced. Marx's inability to complete *Capital* did not permit him to take the final step towards the concrete, which would have been to situate the system of relations he had defined into the world market. This is the context in which several of the problems to which Wallerstein alludes should be posed, except that we would then have a rigorous theoretical formulation and not a merely descriptive or scholarly exercize. This analysis would enable the production of concepts capable of conceiving theoretically the articulation of non-capitalist modes of production within the capitalist world market. Such an analysis would also permit us to decide to what extent this articulation of different modes of production is solely a phenomenon pertaining to the prehistory of capital – as Marx suggests in his theory of primitive accumulation – or whether, on the other hand, it is a permanent structural process throughout the entire history of capitalism. This would enable us, finally, to do justice to the most original intuition contained in the works of Frank and Wallerstein, which these two authors nevertheless distort: the relative autonomy of mercantile forms from the modes of production which sustain them. This mercantile autonomy, all the more notable the less industrial capitalism is developed, constitutes a kind of 'economic bonapartism' that operates between various productive structures, and prevails to the extent that production for the market develops in non-capitalist forms. Now, despite the importance of the phenomenon, we have no *theory* of the relative autonomy of commercial capital prior to capitalism. Current positions have transformed this autonomy into an absolute – seeing in commercial capital a dissolvent of the feudal order – or have denied it totally – postulating the complete subordination of commercial capital to the dominant mode of production. Between these two extremes lies a theoretical vacuum which needs to be filled.

If the Frank-Wallerstein tendency has come to deny the theoretical significance of the concepts of various modes of production and to transfer all significant theoretical determination to economic systems, the last decade has also seen a contrary tendency – a theoretical inflation of the concept of mode of production to a point where the specific level of economic systems disappears altogether. Thus in Latin America the concept of 'colonial mode of production' has gained some currency. The phenomenon of colonialism – a structural relation between various parts of the world economy which by definition belongs to the analytical level of economic systems – is illegitimately transferred to the level of modes of production. As Enrique Tandeter has rightly pointed out in a recent article tracing the intellectual history of the idea, this theoretical error was linked to the peculiar reception of Althusserianism in Latin America. This reception occurred at a moment when the critique of Frank's circulationism had awoken a new and unexpected interest in the study of Latin American modes of production, but was seriously compromized by a failure to bear in mind the abstract character of the concept of mode of production. The result was that any 'empirical' differentiation was considered sufficient to announce *urbi et orbi* the discovery of a new mode of production. This mistake was doubtless facilitated by ambiguities inherent in the initial formulation of Althusser's theory. Tandeter writes: 'This innovation was at the same time an impoverishment, the basic reason for which lay in the very sense of the Althusserian interpretation of Marxism. It is sufficient in this context to cite Balibar's precise self-criticism on a basic point. Thus, Balibar writes that in 1967–8 he had not understood that "there is no real historical dialectic which is not the process of transformation of every concrete 'social formation'", that is to say, that "'social formations' are not simply the 'concrete' site (or means) *in* which is realized a general abstract dialectic" and that these formations "are in reality the *only* object which is transformed, because it is the only one which really implies a history of class struggle." The mistake of 1967–8 is summarized, then, as "instead of dealing with social formations, *only* modes of production were considered, that is, a still abstract generality of which, in practice, social formations appeared only as the particular and concrete "realization"'.[7]

The theory of 'colonial modes of production' was to be an outstanding example of this illegitimate transposition of levels. Ciro Cardoso, one of the first to formulate it,[8] speaks of a 'colonial slave mode of production' and finds the following as its defining features *at the level of mode of production*: 1) the fact that the slave in Latin America 'had his own economy, based on the proprietor's concession of the produce of a plot of land'; 2) the fact that in Latin America slavery developed in social formations that were dependent, peripheral and deformed; 3) the fact that in Latin America slaves came from populations of a lower level of development than those of Europeans and those belonging to different 'races'. These three features, by which he attempts to define the difference between Ancient slavery and American colonial slavery, are considered by Cardoso sufficient to speak of different modes of production in these two cases. As we can see, the result is to dissolve the concept of mode of production once again, albeit for reasons contrary to those of Wallerstein. In the case of the latter, the concept is dissolved because all its essential determinants are transferred to the level of economic systems; in the case of the former, because even the most secondary empirical variations are regarded as sufficient for us to discover different modes of production, which opens up the possibility of reproducing them *ad infinitum.* Where do we draw the line? For Cardoso there is no theoretical criterion: merely the social scientist's empirical assessment of what is relevant. Yet, of course, there are far greater differences between an 18th century workshop in Manchester and a large modern corporation than between Ancient slavery and American colonial slavery.

[7] E. Tandeter, 'Sobre el análisis de la dominación colonial', *Desarrollo Economico*, Buenos Aires, vol. 16, no 61, Abril–Junio 1976.

[8] 'Sobre los modos de produccion coloniales en America Latina'; 'El Modo de Produccion esclavista colonial en America'; 'Severo Martinez Pelaez y el carácter del regimen colonial', in Assadourian, Cardoso, Ciafardini, Garavaglia y Laclau, *Modos de produccion en America Latina,* Córdoba, 1973.

Why call the former 'capitalist' then, rather than speaking of two different modes of production? Once this course is adopted, concepts disintegrate as theoretical categories and analysis lapse into a vulgar empiricism.

We may conclude from these twin errors then, that it is urgent that Marxist theory differentiate modes of production and economic systems as different levels of analysis – the second constituting a more concrete level which presupposes the first. To perpetuate confusion of the two cannot but lead to the multiplication of pseudo-problems and paradoxes.

2

The Specificity of the Political

Nicos Poulantzas's work *Political Power and Social Classes*[1] is of considerable theoretical importance in at least two senses: in the first place, because Marxist thought did not begin to develop, until the last decade, a systematic theory about the nature and the role of the State in various socio-economic formations. Sketchy observations attempting to establish the *ultimate* coherence between socio-economic changes and the transformations of the political system, or not so sketchy observations attempting to establish mechanical relations of causality between the two, have dominated the area of analysis to such a point that we can only welcome a work which tries to establish on the theoretical level the specificity of the political and which *systematically* avoids purely impressionistic correlations. But, in the second place, the work of Poulantzas is not a simple Marxist work. It appears within a perfectly defined theoretical ambit within the currents of contemporary Marxism: that constituted by the 'Althusserian revolution'. *Political Power and Social Classes* constitutes, without doubt the most complete attempt so far to construct a *regional theory*, starting from the general problematic of Althusser. In this way, it constitutes, up to a certain point, a test of the fruitfulness of this problematic for the analysis of concrete processes and situations. We must, in this respect, bear in mind that a theoretical approach is fruitful to the extent that it is revealed as a multiplier of spontaneous creativity arising in particular areas which could not have fully developed for lack of a prin-

[1] *Political Power and Social Classes*, London, NLB, 1973. Reprinted 1975, 1976, 1977.

ciple of systematization, that is to say, the possibility of theoretical incorporation into the framework of a problematic. A narrow or inadequate problematic, on the contrary, hides the true problems instead of clarifying them, and creates an insuperable antagonism between general theoretical formulations and the knowledge of particular ambits and concrete situations.

On both these counts: its originality as an attempt to formalize theoretically the specificity of the political, and its relationship with the Althusserian problematic – to which we must add the indubitable rigour and theoretical sophistication with which the attempt has been carried out – Poulantzas' work has been, and will presumably continue to be at the very centre of contemporary Marxist political analysis. It will be necessary, elsewhere, to make an overall analysis of Poulantzas' thought. In this essay, however, the aim will be a more limited one: to consider some of the theoretical implications of the debate carried on by Poulantzas and Miliband in *New Left Review*[2] after the publication of Miliband's book *The State in Capitalist Society*.[3]

We will begin, then, by summarizing the general lines of the debate. Poulantzas' first attack arises from an epistemological critique of Miliband's method of analysis. This method consists substantially of the following: starting from a current assertion of bourgeois political science, demonstrating that the facts are in contradiction to it and concluding, therefore, that the assertion is false. In short, Miliband's whole analysis remains on an empirical plane: it starts with assertions referring to reality and it proves that reality is in contradiction with those assertions. It is precisely the validity of this approach that Poulantzas goes on to criticize: 'Instead of *displacing* the epistemological terrain and submitting these ideologies to the critique of Marxist science by demonstrating their inadequacy

[2] N. Poulantzas, 'The Problem of the Capitalist State', *New Left Review*, no 58, Nov.–Dec. 1969, R. Miliband, 'Reply to Nicos Poulantzas', *New Left Review*, no 59, Jan.–Feb. 1970; R. Miliband, 'Poulantzas and the Capitalist state', *New Left Review*, no 82, Nov.–Dec. 1973. I quote the first two articles from Robin Blackburn ed., *Ideology in Social Sciences*, Fontana/Collins, 1972.

[3] *The State in Capitalist Society*, London, 1969. Reprinted 1975.

to the real (as Marx does, notably in the *Theories of Surplus-Value*), Miliband appears to omit this first step. Yet the analysis of modern epistemology shows that it is never possible simply to oppose "concrete facts" to concepts, but that these must be attacked by other parallel concepts situated in a different problematic. For it is only by means of these new concepts that the old notions can be confronted with concrete reality'.[4]

Briefly, Poulantzas asserts that it is not a valid method to consider the propositions of bourgeois political science in isolation, as empirical propositions, without trying to extricate their theoretical substance and without taking the analysis to the arena of theoretical confrontation. The error corresponding to this attitude is that Miliband does not consider it necessary to make explicit his own epistemological principles and the theoretical proposition by which he judges his opponents, i.e., the Marxist theory of the State, and he then commits the same error in his attack against bourgeois ideologies of the State, placing them on the same terrain. The consequence is that these ideologies end up being introduced into Miliband's own analysis. This is evident: 'in the difficulties that Miliband has in comprehending social classes and the State as *objective structures*, and their relations as *an objective system of regular connections,* a structure and a system whose agents, "men", are in the words of Marx, "bearers" of it – *träger*. Miliband constantly gives the impression that for him social classes or "groups" are in some way reducible to *interpersonal relations,* that the State is reducible to interpersonal relations of the diverse "groups" that constitute the State apparatus, and finally that the relation between social classes and the State is itself reducible to interpersonal relations of "individuals" composing social groups and "individuals" composing the State apparatus. . . . According to this problematic, the agents of a social formation, "men", are not considered the bearers of objective instances (as they are for Marx) but as the genetic principle of the level of the social whole. This is a problematic of *social actors,* of the individuals as the origin of *social action*: sociological research thus leads finally, not to the study of the

[4] Poulantzas, 'The Problem . . .', p. 241.

objective co-ordinates that determine the distribution of agents into social classes and the contradictions between these classes, but to the search for finalist explanations founded in the *motivations of conduct* of the individual actors. This is notoriously one of the aspects of the problematic both of Weber and of contemporary functionalism. To transpose this problematic of the subject into Marxism is in the end to admit the epistemological principles of the adversary and to risk vitiating one's own analysis.'[5]

Poulantzas cites various examples where Miliband's empiricist methodology leads him to the theoretical error mentioned in the above proposition. Thus, in the case of the theory of élites, Miliband attempts to show that their existence is not incompatible with the presence of a ruling class, instead of criticizing the ideological notion of élite in the light of Marxist concepts. In the case of managerialism, his critique of the ideological conception of a 'managerial revolution' consists of showing that managers seek profit as much as any other economic élite forming part of the ruling class, without seeing that the category of profit is an objective category independent of the motivation of conduct of its bearers, and without referring to the really relevant problem which is that of the relations between different fractions of capital. Miliband also fails in his consideration of the bureaucracy since he focuses his analysis on the social origins and personal ties of bureaucrats with members of the ruling class, i.e., citing the *class situation* and not the *objective function* of the bureaucracy as the relevant factor.

This constant diversion from the objective structures and laws of the system to the personal motivations of their agents – which is a consequence of the one-sided emphasis of Miliband, concerned with the empirical validity of the propositions of bourgeois ideology and not with their theoretical refutation – is even more obvious, according to Poulantzas, when Miliband tries to formulate general propositions valid for the system as a whole. Thus, the principles which govern the relative predominance of one or other of the branches of the political system would be for Miliband the relative proximity of the mem-

[5] *Ibid.*, pp. 241–2.

bers of that branch to the ruling class, or the immediate economic role of that branch. Miliband's methodology and theoretical outlook hinders him from understanding that : 'The State apparatus forms an *objective system* of special "branches" whose relations present a specific *internal unity* and which obeys, to a large extent, *its own logic. . . . A significant shift* in the predominant branch in the State apparatus, or in the relations between these branches, cannot be directly established by the immediate exterior role of this branch, but is determined *by the modification of the whole system of the state apparatus and of its form of internal unity as such*: a modification which is itself due to changes in the relations of production and to developments in the class struggle.'[6] In the same way, the changes in the present stage of the capitalist State would be related to the ever closer links between members of the ruling class and the State apparatus, rather than with objective changes in the articulation between economy and polity. In this respect Miliband's thesis approximates to the orthodox Communist thesis of *State monopoly capitalism.* Finally, Miliband has not noticed – although Poulantzas criticizes himself also for partially making the same error – that ideologies also constitute an objective and institutionalized system, comprizing the Church, political parties, professional associations (with the exceptions of the revolutionary party and the trade unions), schools, the mass media and the family. In this sense Poulantzas talks of ideological State apparatuses along with repressive State apparatuses.

The first reply from Miliband was rather cautious and defensive. He tried to justify his method without entering into open confrontation with Poulantzas' conception by limiting the difference to a problem of emphasis. Thus he writes, 'I would readily grant that *The State in Capitalist Society* may be insufficiently "theoretical" in the sense in which Poulantzas means it; but I also tend to think that his own approach . . . errs in the opposite direction. . . . This, I must stress, is not a crude (and false) contraposition of empiricist versus non- or anti-empiricist approaches: it is a matter of emphasis – but the emphasis is important.'[7] Miliband does, however, make an

[6] *Ibid.*, p. 248.
[7] Miliband, 'Reply . . .', pp. 255–6.

assertion of prime importance for the future course of the debate: 'In fact, I quite explicitly give an outline of the Marxist theory of the State but undoubtedly do so very briefly. One reason for this . . . is that, having outlined the Marxist theory of the State, I was concerned to set it against the dominant democratic-pluralist view and to show the latter deficiencies *in the only way in which this seems to me to be possible, namely in empirical terms* (my emphasis, EL).'[8]

The same tendency to reduce the dimensions of his confrontation with Poulantzas to a question of emphasis can be found in Miliband's reply concerning the problem of the theoretical status of political élites and managerialism. The axis of his reply turns, however, around the objective nature of the State. Here his position is clear: to conceive of the State exclusively as a system of objective relations leads to a structural superdeterminism which prevents us from establishing on the theoretical level the relative autonomy of the capitalist State. It is worth quoting this paragraph in full since it constitutes the core of his argument: 'For what his (Poulantzas') *exclusive* stress on "objective relations" suggests is that what the State does is in every particular and at all times *wholly* determined by these "objective relations": in other words, that the structural constraints of the system are so absolutely compelling as to turn those who run the State into the merest functionaries and executants of policies imposed upon them by "the system". At the same time, however, he also rejects the "long Marxist tradition (which) has considered that the State is only a simple tool or instrument manipulated at will by the ruling class" (p. 74). Instead he stresses "the relative autonomy of the State". But all that seems to me to do is to substitute the notion of "objective structures" and "objective relations" for the notion of "ruling class". But since the ruling class is a dominant element of the system, we are, in effect, back at the point of total subordination of the State élite to that class; i.e., the state is not "manipulated" by the ruling class into doing its bidding: it does so autonomously but totally because of the "objective relations" imposed upon it by the system. Poulantzas condemns the "economism" of the Second and Third

[8] *Ibid.*, p. 254.

Internationals and attributes to it their neglect of the State (p. 68). But his own analysis seems to me to lead straight towards a kind of structural determinism, or rather a structural superdeterminism, which makes impossible a truly realistic consideration of the dialectical relationship between the state and the system.'[9]

This structural superdeterminism leads, according to Miliband, to the obliteration of differences between different forms of government and the bourgeois State. According to this conclusion, there would be no real difference between a bourgeois 'democracy' and a fascist State – a conception which constituted the central error of the Comintern during the inter-war period. The very disregard by Poulantzas for the differences between various forms of government leads him to an erroneous treatment of the phenomenon of Bonapartism, which he presents as characteristic of *all* forms of the capitalist State when actually it has emerged only in exceptional circumstances. Finally, he rejects the notion that the ideological State apparatuses belong to the system of the State.

Miliband's reply is, as a whole, unsatisfactory: on one hand he tries to reduce the conflicts to a problem of emphasis, and on the other his methodological assertions and his theoretical criticisms suggest that his differences with Poulantzas go much further than this supposed difference of emphasis would seem to indicate.

Three years later, however, in a new article published to mark the appearance of the English edition of Poulantzas' book, he re-opens the debate with a new, much more elaborated and far-reaching attack. Poulantzas' conception, formerly characterized as *structural superdeterminism*, is now conceived as *structuralist abstractionism*. By this we should understand, if I have correctly interpreted Miliband – a theoretical approach in which an abstractly defined instance seeks its explanatory principle in another, equally abstractly defined instance, but in such a way that this process of referring one instance to the other turns into a circular procedure or a game of mirrors in which finally, nothing has a precise meaning and the conceptual system as a whole is contradictory. The conse-

[9] *Ibid.*, p. 258–9.

quence of this, according to Miliband, is that Poulantzas is unable to answer the very problems that he poses, and he is particularly incapable of giving an answer to the central problem: the relative autonomy of the capitalist State. The self-contradictory method of structuralist abstractionism itself leads Poulantzas to reintroduce economism, after having made the denunciation of it a point of principle. Miliband asserts: 'Poulantzas tells us that "power is not located in the level of structure, but is an effect of the ensemble of these levels, while at the same time characterizing each of the levels of the class struggle." From this proposition ... Poulantzas moves on to the idea that the "concept of power cannot thus be applied to one level of the structure. When we speak for example of *state power,* we cannot mean by it the mode of the state's articulation at the other levels of the structure; *we can only mean the power of a determinate class* to whose interests (rather than those of other social classes) the state corresponds". Now this, I should have thought, is manifestly incorrect: it is simply not true that by "state power" we can only mean "the power of a determinate class". For this, *inter alia,* is to deprive the State of any kind of autonomy at all and to turn it *precisely* into the merest instrument of a determinate class – indeed all but conceptualize it out of existence.'[10]

The reason for this confusion, according to Miliband, is that Poulantzas has not established a vital distinction: that between *state power* and *class power.* 'State power is the main and ultimate – but not the only – means whereby class power is assured and maintained. But one of the main reasons for stressing the importance of the notion of the relative autonomy of the state is that there is a basic distinction between class power and state power, and that the analysis of the meaning and implications of that notion of relative autonomy must indeed focus on the forces which cause it to be greater or less, the circumstances in which it is exercized, and so on. The blurring of the distinction between class power and state power by Poulantzas makes any such analysis impossible: for all the denunciations of "economism", politics does here assume an "epiphenomenal" form.'[11]

[10] Miliband, 'Nicos Poulantzas . . .', p. 87.
[11] *Ibid.*, pp. 87–8.

From this confusion follows a whole series of inadequacies in Poulantzas' analysis: from the erroneous conception of the ideological state apparatuses to his no less erroneous conception of political parties, reduced to being unable to play any autonomous organizational role. From this follows a particularly convincing critique of the conception of Bonapartism in Poulantzas.

Let us begin, then, an analysis of the theoretical structure of this polemic. In the first place we will have to take up some of the methodological questions.

Methodological and Epistemological Questions

Poulantzas began by stating the *theoretical* inadequacy of Miliband's method and, we must point out, he received no reply on this count. On the one hand, it is not possible to consider Miliband's impressionistic observations about differing points of emphasis as a reply. On the other hand, although Poulantzas' assertion that 'it is never possible to oppose "concrete facts" to concepts situated in a different problematic' is formally contradicted by Miliband when he says that he has tried 'to show the deficiencies (of the democratic pluralist view) in the only way which seems to me possible, namely in empirical terms', Miliband makes no attempt whatsoever to justify this assertion; everything depends on defining what is understood by 'empirical terms'. If by this we understand an instance external to thought, whose function is to test the validity of a theory, we find ourselves fully within an empiricist framework and the critique of Poulantzas is vindicated. If, however, the 'concrete facts' are produced by the theory or problematic itself – as modern epistemology asserts – then the problems of logical consistency and empirical validity are not substantially different. The 'forms of proof' of the validity of assertions relating to the object of knowledge can only be considered external to the theoretical system in question if one admits the identification between 'object of knowledge' and 'real object', and the consequent distinction between subject and object of knowledge. To show the inadequacy between the system of axioms which defines the ambit of a theory and the assertions relating the objects arising within this theory itself is, at the same time, to demonstrate the internal contradictions of the theory. It is for this reason that, strictly speaking, the 'empirical validity' and the 'theoretical validity' of a theory are not aspects which can be differentiated. Now then, if Miliband understood his task as an effort to show the internal contradictions of a theoretical problematic starting from the 'facts' arising within it, the theoretical exercise could be justified. But, on the contrary, everything in his line of argument is presented as if his appeal to the 'facts' was a direct appeal to real objects. This is not just a difference of emphasis with Poulantzas, but a radically different epistemological position. Furthermore, the whole polemic takes its course as though Miliband had not noticed the importance of this first disagreement.

We should point out, in this respect, that theoretical practice takes place wholly on the plane of thought. As Althusser has pointed out, the process of knowledge does not begin with real objects – as empiricism supposes – but with concepts, pieces of information and ideas provided by the different forms of practice: scientific, ideological, technical, etc. These concepts are transformed by theoretical practice into objects of knowledge which, as such, are different from real objects. In contrast to the empiricist analysis, according to which knowledge starts from the concrete and is raised to general propositions through a process of abstraction/generalization, we accept the epistemological perspective that knowledge is knowledge *of* real objects but occurring wholly on the level of thought and moving from the abstract to the concrete. This 'concrete' is not, however, the real-concrete but the concrete-in-thought, to use Althusser's expression. So, as we were saying before, in so far as the object of knowledge is produced by theoretical practice itself, the methods of verification are part of the theoretical system itself. A theory is only false to the extent that it is internally inconsistent, i.e., if in the process of construction of its concepts it has entered into contradiction with its postulates.

Hence, *theoretical* problems, to the extent that they are truly theoretical cannot, strictly speaking, be *solved*: they can only be *superseded,* which is not the same thing. Let us analyze this assertion more closely: what exactly does it mean to solve a theoretical problem? In the first instance, it means providing a solution to the difficulties arising from the process of applying a general theory to a particular *theoretical* ambit. But then two possibilities exist: the first of these is that the problem is effectively resolved, in the course of scientific analysis, in accordance with the general assumptions of the theory in question, which means that the problem exists not *in the theory* but in ourselves, i.e., in the present level which our development of it has reached. *The empirical resolution of the problem consists, strictly speaking, of the negation of its existence on the theoretical plane.* The other possibility is that the development of a theory leads to the posing of a truly theoretical problem (i.e. one involving an inconsistency in the logical structure of the theory): but if the problem really is theoretical this means that it cannot be resolved within the system of postulates of the theory, that is to say, *that it has no solution.* This suggests that a theory has reached the limit of its possible development and that, consequently, it enters into contradiction with itself. From this point on, the only way forward is to deny the system of axioms on which the theory is based: that is, to move from one theoretical system to another. But as the problem generating this theoretical crisis has emerged and exists only within the theoretical horizon of the previous system it cannot, in this case either, be said to have been solved: it has simply been superseded, it has dissolved as a problem with the emergence of a new theoretical system. From the theoretical system to the theoretical problems and from them to a new theoretical system: that is the course of the process of knowledge.

Now, assuming that the area of empirical confrontation of a theory's system of propositions is not external, but internal to the theory – in that the problematic creates its own objects – the '*empirical*' *verification*, in so far as it disproves the theoretical propositions, demonstrates the internal contradictions of the *theoretical system.* In conclusion, if we admit – without attributing to this admission an apodictic character – that a theoretical critique starts from the 'empirical' confrontation of the theoretical system under consideration, the necessary logical steps would be: (a) to indicate the points of conflict between the sphere or 'empirical' confrontation and the theoretical system in question – bearing in mind that this is far from being a mechanical operation, since it is necessary to carry out the confrontation taking into account the level of abstraction of the proposition (in speaking of abstraction, we do so, of course, in the hypothetico-deductive sense of the term, not in the inductivist sense); (b) starting from the points in discord, to identify the theoretical problems; (c) starting from the theoretical problems, to demonstrate the internal theoretical contradictions which lead to the collapse of the theoretical system; (d) to propose an alternative theoretical system which can overcome the internal contradictions of the previous one.

Returning to the Poulantzas-Miliband debate, I think it becomes clear that Miliband's book, despite its undoubted interest, is of limited theoretical scope, since the analysis does not go beyond step (a). Poulantzas, however, tends to suggest that the critical endeavour is incomplete because steps (b) and (c) are not accomplished ('displacing the epistemological terrain and submitting these ideologies to the critique of Marxist science by demonstrating their inadequacy to the real'); and neither is step (d) ('a precondition of any approach to the concrete is to make explicit the epistemological principles of its own treatment of it').[12]

But according to Poulantzas, Miliband has not only not subjected the ideological conceptions of the adversary to scientific criticism, but by remaining on the terrain of the latter, has ended up incorporating 'uncritically' those very conceptions. This, he says, is reflected in the predominance, in Miliband's conception, of a problematic of the subject, in which the motivations of the social actors occupy a central role in the explanation of historical change. On this point, however, I feel that Poulantzas' critique has gone a little too far. Miliband's text has not progressed sufficiently into the field of theoretical formalization for us to be able to accept Poulantzas' categorical assertion that Miliband reduces 'the role of the State to the conduct and behaviour of the members of the State apparatus'. Miliband's text permits of different readings – for example, that the links between members of the State apparatus and members of the ruling class are an *indication* of class domination and not its cause.

[12] I do not wish to imply by this that Poulantzas would agree with the whole of my previous schema.

The Method of Poulantzas

Accepting that Miliband's book remains in the prehistory of theoretical formalization, what do we make of Poulantzas' work, which is an attempt to orient explicitly in this direction? I think that, in this respect, the results are far from satisfactory. Not so much for the reasons pointed out by Miliband, i.e., an inadequate empirical enquiry, but exactly the opposite: because of the lack of theoretical confrontation with the problematic of his adversaries. Poulantzas does not try to demonstrate the internal contradictions of the problematics which he rejects and the form in which his own problematic supersedes those contradictions, but confines himself to *describing* the points of discrepancy and carrying straight on. Let us look at an example. Poulantzas quotes texts from Marx relating to the formation of the proletariat and the distinction between class-in-itself and class-for-itself and concludes: 'One reading of these texts must be rejected from the start, for it is connected with the problematic of the "social group" which has no place in Marx's analysis: this is the historico-genetic reading'.[13] Further on, even more emphatically: 'This reading of Marx's analysis is itself related to a historicist problematic: it must be pointed out here that it is precisely in the theory of classes that its inadequacy is most clearly revealed.'[14]

There follows a description of the theory of classes in two variants of the historicist problematic: Lukács, and the functionalist interpretations of Marx (Geiger, Dahrendorf, Bourdieu). How is this inadequacy of the historicist problematic revealed in the theory of classes? The answer comes two pages later: 'This conception fails to recognize two essential facts: firstly, that the agents of production, for example the wage-earning labourer and the capitalist, as "personifications" of Wage-labour and Capital, are considered by Marx as the *supports* or *bearers* of an ensemble of structures; secondly, that social classes are never *theoretically* conceived by Marx as the genetic origin of structures, inasmuch as the problem concerns the definition of the *concept* of class. We shall see why'.[15]

[13] Poulantzas, '*Political Power* . . .', p. 60.
[14] *Op. cit.*, loc. cit.
[15] *Op. cit.*; p. 62.

But this does not demonstrate that the historicist problematic reveals its inadequacy in the theory of classes, it only reveals its inadequacy in relation to the problematic of Poulantzas. That two different conceptions of the same reality may oppose each other is not surprising. The important task would have been to show the internal contradictions of the historicist problematic regarding the theory of classes, that is to say, to have detected the theoretical problems and traced the course which leads from the theoretical problems to the crisis of the problematic and to show, finally, how the anti-historicist problematic is free from these types of contradictions. The above quotation concludes with a 'We shall see why'. But what we see from here on is the development of Poulantzas' theory concerning social classes, without the slightest attempt at criticism of the historicist currents other than a statement of the differences. The same procedure is followed in the analysis of ideologies and bureaucracy and, in general, throughout Poulantzas' work.

Returning to our previous analysis, we could say that if Miliband has started and remains throughout his whole analysis in stage (a), Poulantzas starts his analysis and remains throughout in stage (d). Stages (b) and (c) appear in his analysis only in a formal way, since his critique of opposing problematics consists not of the determination of their internal contradictions but of a simple description of the differences which they express with regard to his own problematic. What is lacking in Poulantzas is a dialectical conception of the process of knowledge, for this conception is incompatible with the idea of problematics as closed universes, unconnected with the internal contradictions of the previous problematics.

Structural Superdeterminism?

Let us consider from this perspective Miliband's criticisms of Poulantzas. The theoretical perspective of the latter has been called by Milibrand structural superdeterminism in his first article and structuralist abstractionism in the second. The first critique referred to the content and the second to the method of creating the concepts (not only to the method of analysis). Miliband's first critique seems to me particularly erroneous and misdirected, not with regard to the appellation structural superdeterminism – which may be correct – but when he maintains that this structural superdeterminism prevents Poulantzas from correctly posing the problem of the relative autonomy of the State. There exists no incompatibility – as Miliband seems to think – between the objective character of the relation existing between the bourgeois class and the State – 'the structural constraints of the system' – and the relative autonomy of this very State. From the Poulantzas viewpoint this relative autonomy would be in turn a structural element, that is to say, the result of a particular articulation between the instances corresponding to the mode of production under consideration; in that sense, one more objective determination of the system as a whole. The relative autonomy of the State and its objective determination would be incompatible only if this autonomy were understood as a break in the chain of necessity and the emergence – however, relative – of a realm of freedom. But this contraposition only makes sense within a problematic of the subject, which Poulantzas excludes by definition. In reality, from having stood his ground on the form in which Miliband seems to understand the relative autonomy of the State, Poulantzas could have found an *a fortiori* argument for strengthening his suspicions of his opponent's 'historicist' propensities. Similarly, I do not think that Miliband's assertion that the structural superdeterminism of Poulantzas must lead necessarily to an indifference towards the various forms of State and government is a valid one. It only leads to a structural explanation of those various forms, which is probably different from the type of explanation that Miliband would give. It would seem that Miliband is working with a simplistic contraposition, in which the adjective '*relative*' constitutes a simple restriction to an autonomy conceived in terms of freedom. For Poulantzas, on the contrary, the '*relative*' character of an autonomy indicates that it belongs to a world of structural determinations, and it is only within this, as a particular moment of it, that the concept of autonomy must be elaborated. Apart from this, the excellent book by Poulantzas *Fascism and Dictatorship*[16] is the most eloquent

[16] NLB, London, 1974.

proof that its author is well aware of the range of differences in the forms of State to which Miliband refers.

With respect to the problem of Bonapartism, I agree with Miliband that Marx and Engels never considered this as a phenomenon characteristic of all forms of State; it is, on the contrary, an exceptional form. As Miliband has clearly pointed out: 'Bonapartism is not the religion of the bourgeoisie at all – it is a last *resort* in conditions of political instability so great as to present a threat to the maintenance of the existing social order, including of course the system of domination which is the central part of that order'.[17] I think, however, that the obvious textual abuse of Poulantzas results from his attempt to grapple with a problem which seems neglected in Miliband's analysis, even at the empirical level: that of the relation between the fraction which retains State power and the dominant classes. Doubtless Miliband would protest, asserting that a good part of his book is precisely devoted to the treatment of this problem; this is true, but he does it from the opposite perspective: trying to show the unity between the two. This problem – the factual processes through which the connection between dominant class and groups holding power are established – is, for Poulantzas, a minor problem: for him the unity of the system is a unity based on objective structures and the central problem is, starting from a general objective determination, to construct in structural terms the concept of the relative autonomy of the various levels. In short, Miliband is interested in determining the *concrete* channels which *in Western Europe* establish the link between fractions which hold political power and dominant classes, and in that sense he emphasizes the elements of unity between the two. Poulantzas, by contrast, is interested in determining, *at the theoretical level,* the autonomous character of the political *within the capitalist mode of production,* and in that sense he emphasizes the elements of separation between dominant class and fraction holding power. The conclusion seems evident: they are analyzing different problems. However, this does not seem apparent to either of the two authors, and consequently, Poulantzas thinks that Miliband has so emphasized the link between

[17] Miliband, 'Nicos Poulantzas . . .', p. 91.

dominant class and elite in power that he can only concede the relative autonomy of the State in the case of fascism – which is false – and Miliband considers that Poulantzas has so emphasized the regimes of exception that he has lost all interest in the bourgeois-democratic form of State or, which is worse, that he sees no difference between the two forms. This supposition of Miliband is also wrong. What happens in the last respect is, firstly, that the terms of the problem analyzed by Poulantzas are reflected more clearly in 'authoritarian' capitalist regimes than in parliamentary ones, and in that sense it is natural to resort to them when seeking examples; secondly, Poulantzas' book does not refer solely to Western Europe but to the capitalist mode of production in general, and on this level, it could perhaps be said that the 'regimes of exception' are the rule.

The Ideological State Apparatuses

Finally, with regard to the 'ideological State apparatuses', I agree completely with Miliband that the problem is badly posed. Poulantzas had begun by asserting that 'inside the structure of several levels dislocated by uneven development the State has the general function of constituting the factor of cohesion of a social formation'.[18] But later, the basic reason which he gives for justifying his conception of the ideological State apparatuses is this: 'If the State is defined as the instance that maintains the cohesion of a social formation and which reproduces the conditions of production of a social system by maintaining class domination, it is obvious that the institution in question – the State ideological apparatus – fills exactly the same function.'[19] There is here a subtle transposition which goes from defining the State as *the instance* which constitutes the factor of cohesion between the levels of a social formation to the assertion that *everything* that contributes to the cohesion of a social formation pertains, by definition, to the State. But in this case Poulantzas' list would be a short one: the reformism of trade unions and social-democratic leaders constitutes a factor of cohesion, and consequently those leaders would be State functionaries; socialist parties would be divided between

[18] Poulantzas, *Political Power* . . ., p. 44.
[19] Poulantzas, 'The problem . . .', pp. 251–2.

a State wing and a revolutionary wing and also, *reductio ad absurdum*, the mind of every individual would be schizophrenically divided between a State half, tending to the cohesion of the social formation and an anti-State half tending to its disruption. Is this not an extreme example of overpoliticization of the various levels of a structure, a historicist deviation against which Poulantzas warns us?

Recently Althusser also has spoken of 'ideological State apparatuses', and has tried to defend this term. But his defence is limited to refuting a possible critique based on the private character of many of the institutions termed. Thus he asserts: 'But someone is bound to question the second, asking me by what right I regard as Ideological *State* Apparatuses, institutions which for the most part do not possess public status, but are quite simply *private* institutions. As a conscious Marxist, Gramsci already forestalled this objection in one sentence. The distinction between the public and the private is a distinction internal to bourgeois law, and valid in the (subordinate) domains in which bourgeois law exercises its "authority". The domain of the State escapes it because the latter is "above the law": the State, which is the State *of* the ruling class, is neither public or private; on the contrary, it is the precondition for any distinction between public and private. The same thing can be said from the starting point of or State Ideological Apparatuses. It is unimportant whether the institutions in which they are realized are "public" or "private. What matters is how they function. Private institutions can perfectly well "function" as Ideological State Apparatuses.'[20]

However the problem persists. It is not a question of whether the institutions are public or private – although on this point Althusser is absolutely correct – it is the fact that, implicit in the conception of 'ideological State apparatuses' there lies a conception of the State which entirely ceases to consider it as an institution (i.e. as an objective structure). Althusser states that 'To my knowledge, *no class can hold State power over a long period without at the same time exercising its hege-*

[20] Louis Althusser, *Lenin and Philosophy and Other Essays*, London, NLB, 1971, pp. 137–8.

mony over and in the State Ideological Apparatuses (Althusser's emphasis).'[21] If the correct statement that a class cannot maintain itself in power for a long period of time without controlling the ideological apparatuses is sufficient for these apparatuses to be considered as belonging to the State, it is because Althusser is accepting a conception of the State identical to that of Poulantzas: *everything* which serves to maintain the cohesion of a social formation forms part of the State. In that case, however, we cannot speak of the State as an *instance* – as in the initial formulation of Poulantzas. The State must simply be a *quality* which pervades all the levels of a social formation. Following this line of reasoning, we witness the dissolution of the notion of State as an objective structure. However, I believe, on the contrary, that the distinction which Miliband establishes between *class power* and *state power* is entirely appropriate, and restores the problem to its true location. The drawback is, of course, that the problem, although correctly located, is not solved. What indeed is *class power* external to *state power*? What is the specificity of the latter? These are questions which remain open.

Structuralist Abstractionism?

We must now pass on to the second of Miliband's characterizations of Poulantzas' theoretical approach: *structuralist abstractionism.* The substance of this method is a type of abstraction which leads to a growing formalism, as a result of which the theoretical substance dissolves into a system of verbal antinomies. I think that this criticism is to a great extent correct; its accuracy is revealed among other things by the predominance of descriptive categories in Poulantzas' theoretical system. Let us be clear, in the first place, that we are using the expression 'formalism' not in the usual epistemological sense, which is associated with the deductive method, but in accordance with the current use of the word, meaning an increasing predominance of form over content. As the theoretical substance of a concept tends to become diluted, the symbolic functions of that concept within the discourse

[21] *Op. cit.*, p. 139.

tend to increase. This happens because no concept occurs in isolation, but as a part of a system. The relations between the different concepts making up that system can be of two kinds: (a) a relation logically interlinking the concepts one with another and tending to stress their theoretical nature; we then have a process of feedback whereby the theoretical function of the concepts tends to become stressed by reason of the logical character of the relations which link them; (b) a relation which is purely descriptive of proximity between different concepts. In the latter case the concept in question also forms part of a system, but this system is a descriptive unity and not a logical structure. But, as each isolated concept *evokes* the descriptive unity of which it forms a part, it is transformed into a symbol of that unity. In this case, the theoretical function of the concepts tends to diminish and their symbolic function tends to increase. A conceptual structure in which the symbolic values of its terms predominate over their theoretical structure we call 'formalism', thus giving it a meaning exactly opposite to that normally understood in epistemology: i.e. a deductive system in which the symbolic function of the concepts plays no role at all. As can be seen, it belongs to the essence of formalism – in the sense in which we use the term here – to start from purely descriptive relationships between the phenomena to be analyzed. Taxonomy and formalism are complementary aspects of the same theoretical attitude.

Going back to Poulantzas, his attitude when faced with a complex reality is to react with taxonomic fury, and his taxonomy is set at a level of abstraction so high – without always being justified – that the symbolic functions of the concepts necessary tend to predominate; these symbols enter into relationship with each other and create in turn symbols of these relations, and all contact with the original meaning is lost. Without abstraction scientific knowledge is not possible, but my argument is that abstraction, such as practiced by Poulantzas, has gone in the direction of *formalism.* I think that, with Poulantzas, the origin of this formalist tendency in the process of abstraction lies in the fact that mutual contact was established between the initial elements of the process of analysis in a purely descriptive way; the result is that in the later stages of the process of abstraction, it is impossible to establish a logical link between these elements. The way out of this dilemma for Poulantzas is the postulation of purely formal relations between the objects of analysis and an increasing use of metaphors. From this point on, abstraction can only be exercized, *necessarily,* in a formalist direction. In Poulantzas' case the worst abuses of this method are avoided because of his acute sensitivity to historical reality. His analyses – such as those of fascism – are often penetrating and thought-provoking, but this result is achieved despite, not because of his method.

Several examples of Poulantzas' formalist theoretical attitude could be mentioned. One is provided by Miliband himself: '"A class," he (Poulantzas) says, "can be considered as a distinct and autonomous class, as a social force, inside a social formation, only when its connection with the relations of production, its economic existence, is reflected on the other levels by a specific presence". . . . One must ask what is a "specific presence"? The answer is that "this presence exists when the relation to the relations of production, the place in the process of production, is reflected on the other levels by *pertinent effects*". What then are "pertinent effects"? The answer is that "we shall designate by 'pertinent effects' the fact that the reflection of the place in the process of production on the other levels constitutes a *new element* which cannot be inserted in the typical framework which these levels would present without these elements". This might be interpreted to mean that a class assumes major significance when it makes a major impact upon affairs – which can hardly be said to get us very far. But Poulantzas does not even mean that. For he also tells us, "The dominance of the economic struggle . . . does *not* mean 'an absence of 'pertinent effects' at the level of the political struggle" – it only means "a certain form of political struggle, which Lenin criticizes by considering it as ineffectual". So, at one moment a class can only be considered as distinctive and autonomous if it exercises "pertinent effects", i.e. a decisive impact; next moment, these "pertinent effects" may be "ineffectual".'[22]

[22] Miliband, 'Nicos Poulantzas . . .', p. 86–7.

The Concept of Mode of Production

Many more of these examples could be quoted. However, I believe that more important than the obvious formalism exemplified by paragraphs like the above, is the way in which this very theoretical attitude affects some of the central theoretical concepts used by Poulantzas, such as the concept of *mode of production*. The criticism of Poulantzas on this score can be applied equally to the use made of the same concept by the whole of the Althusserian current. Poulantzas, following Balibar in this, asserts: 'By *mode of production* we shall designate not what is generally marked out as the economic . . . but as a specific combination of various structures and practices which, in combination, appears as so many instances and levels, i.e. as so many regional structures of this mode. . . . Furthermore, the fact that the structure of the whole is determined in the last instance by the economic does not mean that the economic always holds the *dominant role* in the structure. The unity constituted by the structure in dominance implies that every mode of production has a dominant level or instance; but the economic is in fact dominant only insofar as it attributes the dominant role to one instance or another, insofar as it regulates the shift of dominance which results from the decentration of the instances . . . Therefore what distinguishes one mode of production from another and consequently specifies a mode of production is the particular form of articulation maintained by its levels: this articulation is henceforth referred to by the term *matrix* of a mode of production.'[23]

This conception tries to take account of two facts which are apparently contradictory: the primacy of the mode of production in material life as a determinant factor of all social life, and the difficulty in assigning to strictly economic factors a directly determinant role in the regulation of historical processes other than the capitalist one. It is, as we know, an old problem. Althusserianism thinks however, it can solve it with its characteristic method: the combination of taxonomy and formalism. It begins by identifying three basic characters: the economic, political and ideological instances, which are pres-

[23] Poulantzas, *Political Power . . .*, pp. 13–15.

ent in all modes of production and whose articulation constitutes the specificity of that mode. Why only three? What has been the method of their deduction? Does there exist any logical link between them? The response is silence to the first two questions and in the negative to the third – the only relation is their articulation, which depends on the mode of production in question. That is to say, we find ourselves with three instances established in a purely descriptive way. It is not then surprising that the relations between these three characters are formal ones: these relations have names assigned to them, but there are no conceptual categories which correspond to these names. In other words, these names are symbols of the real objects to which they refer, but not theoretical concepts which explain the nature of those realities. The names of the relations are: 'determination in the last instance by the economic' and 'dominant role', understanding by the first that the economic decides which instance has to have the dominant role in each mode of production. But these are metaphors, which only make sense by analogy with other metaphors. At this altitude we are now in the realm of complete mythology, in an abstract world of structures and levels in which it becomes impossible to establish logical relations between the concepts.

Let us try to prove these assertions in a more explicit way. According to Balibar, some of the concepts used by Marx suffer from the defect of being theoretically only half-formalized: on the one hand they continue partly to be prisoners of a prior ideological problematic; on the other, they indicate the theoretical location of a solution without being able to think it theoretically: 'I think, on the contrary, that within theoretical practice itself, this text [the Preface to *A Contribution to a Critique of Political Economy*] has the status of what is called a set of *practical* concepts. In other words, this text offers us concepts which still depend in their *formulations* precisely on the problematic which has to be displaced; at the same time, without being able to think it in its concept they indicate *where we must go* in order to pose otherwise (and at the same stroke solve) a new problem which has arisen within the old problematic.'[24] Confronted with this state of affairs, Balibar

[24] Etienne Balibar in *Reading Capital*, London, NLB, 1970, pp. 204–5.

writes: 'I propose to begin this work here, an explicit labour which *transforms* these *'practical'* concepts into *theoretical* concepts of the Marxist theory of history, a labour which strips them of their present theoretical form in order to make them theoretically adequate to their practical content. At the same time, those concepts which are no more than expressions of the exigencies of the old ideological problematic, will disappear completely. And at the same time, too, weak and open points will appear which will demand the production of new theoretical concepts even in the region explored by Marx, and make this production possible'.[25]

Balibar's theoretical project is unobjectionable. Our criticism is that he has not fully completed it, since in speaking of *the political* and *the economic* he has failed to produce them as *theoretical concepts* and has got stuck half way between theoretical comprehension and purely descriptive relationships. Let us quote the text from Marx on which both Balibar and Poulantzas base their analysis: 'In all forms in which the direct labourer remains the "possessor" of the means of production and labour conditions necessary for the production of his own means of subsistence, the property relationship must *simultaneously* appear as a direct relationship of lordship and servitude, so that the direct producer is not free; a lack of freedom which may be reduced from serfdom with enforced labour to mere tributary relationship. . . . Under such conditions the surplus-labour for the nominal owner of the land can only be extorted from them *by other than economic pressure*, whatever the form assumed may be. . . . Thus conditions of personal dependence are requisite, a lack of personal freedom, no matter to what extent, and being tied to the soil as its accessory, bondage in the true sense of the word.'[26]

The crux of Balibar's analysis is this notion of 'extra-economic coercion'. We should note, in the first place, that Balibar accepts the notions of 'economic base' or 'economic level' as pure and simple synonyms of 'level of production'. Marx did also. However, Balibar utilizes the notion of 'extra-economic coercion' – which Marx also uses – without noticing

[25] Balibar, *op. cit.*, p. 208.
[26] Marx, *Capital*, vol. III, pp. 771–2.

that it involves a notion of 'the economic' which is incompatible with the first meaning (economy = level of production). For it is obvious that if the extra-economic coercion (i.e. *different* from the economic) constitutes the central element in the relations *of production* and appropriation of surplus-value, the concept of production and the concept of 'the economic' cannot be synonymous. Why is it that in non-capitalist modes of production the coercion *must* be extra-economic? On this question Marx's answer is completely unambiguous: because labour power has not been transformed into a commodity, and, as a result, the exchange of commodities does not yet constitute the basis of the relations of production. Therefore the sphere of the economic – in this second sense – is the sphere of commodities, the market. The emergence of the free labour market is the decisive factor in the appearance of capitalism. In previous modes of production 'the economic' – market relations – also exist, but they have not penetrated the sphere of production, and in that sense, cannot be the 'determinant element in the last instance', to use Balibar's expression.

It is quite clear, then, that Marx is using two different conceptions of 'the economic'. These conceptions are different in two ways: in the first place, in that they are of different levels of abstraction (once again using the notion of 'abstraction' in its hypothetic-deductive sense). The first conception of 'the economic' (= production) belongs to the more general theory of historical materialism in that it defines one of the conditions of every possible society; the second conception, however, only refers to the societies producing commodities. But both concepts differ not only in regard to their level of abstraction, but also in that they do not stand in direct relationship to one another. 'The economic' in the second sense is not a particular case – e.g. *differentia specifica* – of the economic in the first sense. On the contrary, the two concepts belong to different theoretical structures whose unity must be produced by the theory itself. To think the *theoretical* conditions for their unity consists precisely in thinking the peculiarity of a specific mode of production: the capitalist. This is why Marx in *Capital* has to think *separately* the abstract conditions of the labour process and the abstract conditions of commodity production, in order to be able to produce the theoretical concept of 'capitalist mode of production'. If indeed these two conceptions of 'the economic' are to be found in the works of Marx, I do not see the usefulness of continuing to use the same expression to designate both. I suggest, therefore, that we continue to use the term '*the economic*' for the second meaning, whilst for the first we should use the term *production*. In this way, the basic proposition of historical materialism, according with which the mode of production of material life determines all other instances of social life, would not establish the primacy of 'the economic' for non-capitalist modes of production, in that extra-economic coercion would be the basis of relations of production.

My point is that Balibar – and Poulantzas too – have not submitted the notion of 'the economic' to a rigorous theoretical critique, and as a result they have not produced a true theoretical concept, but have proceeded using a descriptive and intuitive concept in which the ambiguity of the two notions we have analyzed persists. Therefore, in relating to a pseudo-object of knowledge, the theoretical analysis becomes weakened and the symbolic meanings increase. In trying to solve the problem within the framework of the Holy Trinity of levels – the economic, the political, the ideological – and not establishing the necessary distinction between *production* and *economy*, Balibar and Poulantzas reduce themselves to a formal game of metaphors such as that 'the economic decides which level is going to have the dominant role' in the same way as a king who reigns but does not rule, until he decides like Louis XIV (just as the capitalist system does) to be his own Prime Minister and to concentrate in his hands the dual condition of determination in the last instance and dominant role. Balibar asserts: '*The economy is determinant in that it determines which of the instances of the social structure occupies the determinant place*. Not a simple relation, but rather a relation between relations; not a transitive causality, but rather a structural causality.'[27]

But it must be one or the other. If by economy we mean the production of material existence, it is not determinant in the last instance but in the first, whatever the mode of production.

[27] Balibar, *op. cit.*, p. 224.

If, on the contrary, we understand 'economy' in the second sense (production of commodities) it has never been determinant except when identified with the basic productive relations of the society. This distinction between the determinant in the last instance and the dominant role seems to be no more than a series of metaphors which attempt to resolve through symbols of little theoretical content, an artificial problem created by the metaphysic of instances. The whole problem arises, we believe, from the predominantly descriptive character in which concepts such as the 'economic' have been introduced into the theoretical discourse. This is, after all, even more the case with concepts such as the 'political' and the 'ideological'. In other words, we have here a new example of the fusion between taxonomy and formalism.

Notice that the problem is not that the three levels should be articulated in a different way and that, consequently, we should attribute to production a political rather than an economic character; what happens is that the separation between the economic and political has not been verified in modes of production prior to capitalism and, therefore, the discrimination between economic and non-economic factors is an artificial operation which projects onto the previous mode of production a type of social rationality existing under capitalism. In that sense, the notion of 'extra-economic coercion' as used by Marx is insufficient because it does not define the coercion in itself, but only its difference from the type of coercion existing under capitalism. This procedure could be justified in *Capital*, since its approximation to non-capitalist modes of production is marginal, destined only to trace the prehistory of capitalism, but it becomes definitely inadequate when we try to advance our understanding of those other modes of production. We should notice, finally, that we are not dealing with a problem of 'relative autonomy' non-existent before capitalism; here Poulantzas confuses the problem. A level can be relatively autonomous from or totally determined by another, but even to be totally determined both must be distinct, and our point is that in most of the cases this distinction would not exist.

Balibar undoubtedly perceives the problem. Thus he states: 'Surplus-labour cannot then be extorted without "other than economic pressure", i.e., without "*Herrschafts- und Knechtschaftsverhältnis*". Even before we have analyzed the 'transformed forms' for themselves, we can conclude that in the feudal mode of production they will not be the transformed forms of the economic base alone. . . . *Not directly economic but directly and indissolubly political and economic*; which means finally, that different modes of production do not combine elements and do not allow differential division and definitions like "the economic", the "legal" and the "political". Historians and ethnologists today often attest the discovery of this effect, though usually in a theoretically blind fashion.'[28] But if different modes of production do not contain homogeneous elements such as 'the economic', 'the juridical' and 'the political', what becomes of the scheme of determination in the last instance by the economic, or of differentiation of modes of production in function of the instance which exercises the dominant role? Above all, what happens to the differentiation between modes of production in function of the different articulation of their elements? It has to be either one or the other: *either* 'the economic', 'the political' and 'the ideological' are so diverse in different modes of production that the only thing linking them is the verbal unity of the name – equivocal concepts, in the Aristotelian sense of the word – and then it is not their articulation which differentiates modes of production from each other, since they come to be strictly incomparable realities; *or*, despite their differences there is an element in common which allows us to attribute to the moment of articulation its differentiating character. If, as Balibar maintains, the 'transformed forms' are not directly economic, but both indissolubly economic and political – with which we agree – we must point out that he has failed to produce *the theoretical concept of this indissolubility* and has substituted for it a symbolic concept – 'determination in the last instance' – which lacks a precise theoretical content.

The possibility of thinking the specificity of modes of production therefore depends on carrying to its logical conclusion the task which Balibar and Poulantzas have set themselves, but have only partially carried out: to eliminate descriptive

[28] *Op. cit.*, p. 223.

categories and replace them by truly theoretical categories. Only thus is it possible to make a cognitive approach to the concrete. If Marx thought the specificity of the capitalist mode of production by *theoretically* linking to the abstract analysis of the labour process the abstract analysis of the process of commodity production, the production of the concepts capable of thinking the specificity of other modes of production should proceed in the same way: by isolating the abstract system of concepts the linking of which could account for the specificity of the mode of production in question. However, if this reasoning is correct, this process can only be verified in so far as the object is really constructed theoretically, and in so far as descriptive, impressionistic or intuitive categories are not allowed to subsist – for these will only succeed in reproducing their ambiguities in the subsequent stages of analysis and will lead to formalism.

In the foregoing pages we have attempted, in a schematic way, to show the theoretical roots of what Miliband has called the structuralist abstractionism of Poulantzas. There are many other aspects which deserve attention in this respect: above all, what seems to be the central deficiency of Poulantzas' approach – its inability to explain, from a theoretical perspective, the process of historical change. However, treatment of these questions goes beyond the aims of this essay, which proposed only to analyze the Poulantzas-Miliband debate. It would be necessary, in order to deal adequately with those questions, to analyze as a whole the positive contributions of Poulantzas to the development of Marxist political thought. This is a task which I consider all the more urgent since I do not agree with the assertion of Miliband that Poulantzas' book 'does not seem to me to be very helpful in the development of Marxist political sociology'. It seems to me, on the contrary, for the reasons given at the beginning of this article, that its importance can hardly be exaggerated.

3

Fascism and Ideology

The most striking thing about Nicos Poulantzas's book *Fascism and Dictatorship*[1] is the exceptional wealth of *theoretical determinations* which he introduces into the analysis of fascism. By this I do not mean that the empirical information it contains is particularly abundant: we have numerous general studies on the fascist period which are more complete than that of Poulantzas, but we find in all of them certain basic deficiencies: either they remain merely at the empirico-descriptive level or, when we burrow down to the historico-explicative mechanisms which order the tangled mass of facts, we find that fascism is reduced to relatively simple contradictions. This situation has been responsible for a certain uneasiness which we experience with regard to the literature on fascism: in the last thirty years this literature has noticeably increased – we know much more of the data relating to the history of fascism – but we have not made a parallel advance in developing the theoretical concepts with which we can understand it. Towards the end of the 1920s Ortega y Gasset wrote: 'Fascism has an enigmatic countenance because in it appears the most counterposed contents. It asserts authoritarianism and organizes rebellion. It fights against contemporary democracy and, on the other hand, does not believe in the restoration of any past rule. It seems to pose itself as the forge of a strong State, and uses means most conducive to its dissolution, as if it were a destructive faction or a secret society. Whichever way we approach fascism we find that it is simultaneously

[1] Nicos Poulantzas, *Fascism and Dictatorship: The Third International and the Problem of Fascism*, London, NLB, 1974. Reprinted 1977.

one thing and the contrary, it is A and not-A . . .'[2]

Somehow, we feel that the enigma has not been totally unravelled, and that even if there is no doubt that fascism was never a revolutionary movement, phenomena such as the mass mobilization that it achieved and the presence in its ideology of elements belonging to the revolutionary tradition have never been convincingly explained. As eloquent proof of this, we only have to remember the high degree to which we still depend for the theoretical understanding of fascism on a few great books written before 1945 – such as those of Guérin,[3] Neumann,[4] Trotsky[5] or Togliatti;[6] and this is despite the abundance of subsequent research which has made many of their analyses obsolete.

I think we have to seek the cause of this deficiency in the fact that nearly all the intellectual and political currents in Europe after 1930 tended not to understand fascism in the complex accumulation of contradictions from which it emerged, but to reduce it to relatively simple contradictions. This was the case, for example, with bourgeois liberal sectors: for them, fascism was not the result of an objective historical process, but an interruption of normal historical development. Thus, for Benedetto Croce,[7] fascism was not the political expression of any class interest, but the result of 'a collapse of conscience, a civil depression and intoxication, produced by the war'. It was not just Italy and Germany, but in one way or another all the countries intervening in the First World War, which shared this sickness. Fascism was, then, a *parenthesis* which had coincided with a reduction in the consciousness of liberty. These three characteristics – moral sickness, universality and parenthesis – conduced to a single result: the impossibility of under-

[2] Jose Ortega y Gasset, 'Sobre el Fascismo', 1927, *Obras Completas,* vol. 11, Madrid, 1954.

[3] Daniel Guérin, *Fascisme et Grand Capital*, Paris, 1936.

[4] F. Neumann, *Behemoth: the Structure and Practice of National Socialism*, New York, 1942.

[5] Trotsky's writings on fascism have recently been collected in the book *The Struggle Against Fascism in Germany*, London, 1975, introduced by Ernest Mandel.

[6] Palmiro Togliatti, *Lezioni sul fascismo*, Rome, 1970, preface by Ernesto Regionieri.

[7] Benedetto Croce, *Scritti e discorsi politici* (1943–7), Bari, 1963, vol. 1, p. 7 et seq; vol. II, p. 46 et seq., and 357 et seq.

standing fascism by means of objective historical categories. The first characteristic cuts short any possible understanding in terms of a class analysis. With the second, fascism is universalized and disconnected from any precise national context. The third asserts the impossibility of understanding it in terms of historical categories, since fascism constituted a *parenthesis* in normal historical development. (Not for nothing did Croce's *History of Italy* – a euphoric idealization of the Giolitti regime – end in 1915). Fascism is explained then, for Croce, as the irruption on the historical scene of almost biological tendencies resulting from the postwar crisis. We would seem to be reading once again Roman historians, a Sallust or a Tacitus, for whom social convulsions were the expression of 'man's' unrestrained instincts in a time when institutions as a whole are breaking up and failing to control them.

This liberal interpretation can certainly be amplified, to the point at which fascism is presented as the culmination of the whole of modern history. For Friedrich Meinecke,[8] for example, fascism constituted a breakdown of the psychic balance between rational and irrational impulses, whose origin must be sought in the lust for gain and material goods aroused by the Enlightenment and modern industrialism. This conception is more 'historical' than that of Croce in appearance only, since although it does not talk of 'parenthesis', the complexity of history intervenes only as a series of circumstances which facilitate or hinder the balance between 'rational' and 'irrational' forces; and these are not, of course, historical products but traits of human nature. Similarly, Catholic liberal interpretations tend to present fascism as a distortion of the natural order of things, a consequence of the excesses initiated by liberalism. Thus, for Maritain, 'By virtue of a reflex action, not human but mechanical, communism arouses and fosters defensive reactions of a fascist or racist type, and these create and foster in turn all the communist defence reactions, so that the two forces multiply and grow simultaneously, one on top of the other: they both make a virtue out of hatred, they

[8] Friedrich Meinecke, *The German Catastrophe*, 1950. A similar confrontation of Croce's and Meinecke's conceptions, as well as a detailed discussion of the different interpretations of fascism, can be found in Renzo de Felice, *Le interpretazioni del fascismo*, Bari, 1969.

are both dedicated to war, war between nations or a war of classes, they both claim for the temporal community the messianic love with which the kingdom of God must be loved, and they both submit man to some inhuman humanism, the atheistic humanism of the dictatorship of the proletariat, or the idolatrous humanism of Caesar, or the zoological humanism of blood and race'.[9] As we see, we can hardly apprehend the specificity of the fascist phenomenon via these analyses, which tend necessarily in the direction of reducing it to a simple contradiction.

This has also occurred with those tendencies which try to explain the roots of fascism in psychological terms. Thus Wilhelm Reich,[10] after pointing out that there exist in man three different layers of biophysical structure – a superficial one in which the average individual is 'restrained, polite, compassionate and conscientious', an intermediate consisting of 'cruel, sadistic, lascivious, predatory and envious impulses' and a 'deepest biological core' in which man is 'an honest, industrious, co-operative animal capable of love and also of rational hatred' – draws the following political conclusion: 'In contradistinction with liberalism, which represents the superficial character layer, and to genuine revolution, which represents the deepest layer, fascism represents essentially the second character layer, that of the secondary impulses'.[11] If one starts from these premises, for which the role of objective historical determinations is reduced to creating the conditions for the predominance of one type of character or another, the conclusion is hardly surprising: 'My medical experience with individuals of all kinds of social strata, races, nationalities and religions showed me that 'fascism' is only the politically organized expression of the average human character structure which has nothing to do with this or that race, nation or party but which is general and international. In this characterological sense "fascism" is the basic emotional attitude of man in authoritarian society, with its machine civilization and

[9] Jacques Maritain, *Humanisme Integral,* Paris, 1936. Quoted by De Felice, *op. cit.*
[10] Welhelm Reich, *The Mass Psychology of Fascism,* London, 1970.
[11] *Op. cit.,* p. XIII.

its mechanistic-mystical view of life.'[12] Similarly, for Erich Fromm,[13] once man has emerged from his undifferentiated identity with nature and becomes more and more an 'individual', he is confronted with a clear alternative: either unite with the world in the spontaneity of love and productive effort, or seek security in the blind adherence to forces outside himself which lead to the destruction of his liberty and of the integrity of his individual self. Fascism, naturally, constitutes for Fromm an extreme form of this second alternative.

We find, then, in all these interpretive schemes, the tendency to explain fascism in terms of the isolated individual and his particular nature.[14] The individual has broken his ties of

[12] *Ibid.*

[13] Erich Fromm, *Fear of Freedom,* London, 1942.

[14] It might seem strange that we attribute to Fromm and Reich a tendency to reduce the fascist phenomenon to mechanisms of individual psychology, given that both authors have insisted that character structure is not fixed once and for all in biological terms, but is the result of a complex determination by social and economic forces. But this does not at all affect our position. In the case of Fromm, the historical process moves in a single and irreversible direction: the progressive break-up of the ties existing between the individual and his traditional forms of insertion in society, and the ambiguous nature of individual liberty that arises from this process. Fascism is only intelligible as a moment in this teleological structure which characterizes modern history as a whole. Furthermore, how did Fromm arrive at this concept of the 'individual'? The operation is carried out in three stages: (1) from the observation that in the present day men appear less linked than in the past to groups of social belonging, one reaches, by simple prolongation *ad quem* of this potential line of development, the concept of 'individual': a man who has broken all ties with his groups of social-belonging; (2) this 'individual', which is no more than a 'concept-limit', a purely imaginary character, is hypostatized and transformed into the *subject* of history: the history of 'man' from the Middle Ages to the present would be the history of the 'individual' and his progressive liberation from social ties, with all the ambiguities and contradictions arising from this process; (3) the beginning of history – feudal society – has a structure as imaginary as its end; further, it is conceived as the antithesis of the latter: the total subsumption of the individual in his groups of social belonging. History as told by Fromm, is therefore a pure mythology from the point of view of its beginning, its end, and the subject which passes from one to the other. Within this theoretical structure one can, of course, insist that the character of the individual is socially and culturally formed, but if we scratch the surface a little we will see that these social and cultural forces are reduced to the basic conflict between individual and society which characterized the whole of modern history. We are dealing then, with a simple contradiction. Even when many of Fromm's psychological observations are correct or suggestive, they seem ideologically deformed by being referred to this mythical subject: the 'individual'. Wilhelm Reich is of a different intellectual stature and one would look in vain in his work for traces of such a simplistic teleology. For Reich too,

social belonging and appears as an undifferentiated mass in the face of the action of demagogues.

These interpretive tendencies which can, up to a point, be explained by their contemporaneity with the historical phenomena they attempt to analyze, were extended and systematized after the war in the theories of 'totalitarianism',[15] which tend to include fascist regimes and the soviet regime under the same heading. For Hannah Arendt, one of the most sophisticated exponents of this tendency, modern totalitarianism arises linked to three essential historical processes: the supersession of the nation State and the emergence of imperialism, the crisis of the class system and its values, and the atomization of the individual in modern mass society. The ideological meaning of this method is clear: it is a sub-product of the cold war which tended to abstract formal features common to both types of regime in order to assert the substantial identity between fascism and communism. What is important for our analysis is that this approach tended, in a new manner, to eliminate the complexity of contradictions constitutive of fascism and to reduce it to one relatively simple contradiction. One of the consequences of this type of approach has been the theoretical inadequacy of analyses of fascism on the part of bourgeois social scientists; in moving within the framework of purely formal 'identities' between totally different regimes, they have been able to do no more than accumulate classifications and subclassifications which are purely descriptive and

---

character is not a biological datum but has been formed by social and cultural forces. But, in the first place, these forces are nothing but the age-long repression of biological needs and impulses. Secondly, fascism is considered the *direct* expression of the resulting character structure. In this way fascism is removed from any concrete conjuncture and comes to be something like the condensation and expression of man's age-old repression accentuated by a particular political and social crisis which has enabled impulses normally sublimated to have a free rein. Only in this way can we explain such statements of Reich as in its pure form fascism is the sum total of all the *irrational* reactions of the average human character' (*op. cit.* p. XIV). Or that 'there is a German, Italian, Spanish, Anglo-Saxon, Jewish and Arabian fascism. *Race ideology is a pure biopathic expression of the character structure of the orgastically impotent man . . .*' (*ibid.*).

[15] cf. especially Hannah Arendt, *The Origins of Totalitarianism,* 1951; C. J. Freidrich, *Totalitarianism,* 1945; M. Bucheim, *Totalitarian Rule: its Nature and Character,* Middletown, 1968; J. L. Talmon, *The Origins of Totalitarian Democracy*, 1952.

devoid of all theoretical interest. The books of Friedrich and Brzezinski, of Organski and of Lipset,[16] are well-known examples of this type of literature. Theorists of 'mass society' – such as Kornhauser and Lederer[17] – have, from another perspective, persisted in a similar approach.

This type of subjectivist aberration has, without doubt, been absent from marxist discussion, where analyses of fascism in terms of 'masses' and the 'adventures of consciousness' of the isolated individual have not developed. But simplification of the analysis of fascism has also operated and continues to operate within Marxism, albeit in a different direction. During the 1920s and early 1930s, there emerged a wealth of marxist studies of fascism which tended to emphasize the multiform variety of contradictions which had led to its emergence. To the works of Trotsky and Togliatti mentioned above, we could add, among others, those of Gramsci, Rosenberg, Thaelheimer and Otto Bauer.[18] But they were insights, preliminary outlines, which needed to be developed and systematized in maturer works. Yet, as the anti-fascist struggle reached a climax, as fascism became more and more the daily enemy in the political practice of millions of militants, a singular thing happened: the quality of the marxist theoretical literature on fascism declined to such a point that, with one notable exception,[19] the late 1930's and the 1940's had nothing to offer remotely comparable to the theoretical richness of the analyses of the earlier period. I think that the reason for this surprising fact lies in the following: while the Comintern had correctly

[16] C. J. Friedrich and Z. K. Brzezinski, *Totalitarian Dictatorship and Autocracy,* Cambridge (Mass.), 1965; A. F. K. Organski, *The Stages of Political Development*; S. M. Lipset, *Political Man: the Social Bases of Politics*.

[17] W. Kornhauser, *The Politics of Mass Society*, London, 1960; E. Lederer, *The State of the Masses,* New York, 1940.

[18] Gramsci's works on fascism have recently been collected in Antonio Gramsci, *Sul fascismo*, a cura di Enzo Santarelli, Rome, 1974; Historicus (pseud. of A. Rosenberg), *Der Faschimus als Massenbewegung,* Carlsbad, 1934; A. Thalheimer, 'Uber den Faschismus', *Gegen den Strom,* nos 2–4, 1930; O. Bauer, *Der Faschismus,* Bratislava, 1936. To these works, centred around European fascism, one should add the study of the Soviet orientalists O. Tamin and E. Yohan, *Militarism and Fascism in Japan*, London, 1934, which is a valuable effort to compare the traits of Japanese and Western European fascism.

[19] The book by Neumann mentioned previously.

appreciated the link between fascism and monopoly capital, the policy of the Popular Fronts initiated in 1935 led to the incorporation of broader and broader sectors of the bourgeoisie into the anti-fascist struggle, with the result that fascism tended to be presented as the political expression of an increasingly reduced sector of interests. In this way, in the analysis of the Comintern, fascism ended up by being the pure and simple expression of a *direct* dictatorship of monopoly capital over the rest of society. Obviously, aspects such as the relative autonomy of the fascist State and the mass mobilization which preceded its coming to power tended to be undervalued. The *authoritarian* character of fascism was put above its character as a *mass regime*; and this naturally coincided with the experience of countries occupied by Hitlerism, which had only been able to appreciate the first aspect. Thus the complexity of fascism was eliminated and reduced to a single contradiction: that existing between monopoly capital and the rest of society. This tendency continued after the war: the broad fronts lauded by the Communist Parties called 'fascist' the potentially authoritarian policies of monopoly capital. Today 'fascist' is applied to regimes like the Chilean Junta, the dictatorship of the colonels in Greece or the regime of the Shah in Iran, which obviously have not the remotest similarity with the regimes of Hitler or Mussolini.[20]

The great merit of Poulantzas's book is that it breaks with this tradition and tries to reopen the theoretical debate suspended in the early 1930's. Fascism is not reduced by Poulantzas to a simple contradiction but is presented, on the contrary, as the result of a very complex over-determination of contradictions. I think it is here that its importance and interest lies, although I disagree with many of its analyses. But before embarking upon a critique, let us indicate the basic features of Poulantzas's interpretation.

[20] This has frequently led to an interpretative ambiguity as far as fascism is concerned, the latter being uncritically attributed the most contradictory meanings. Ernesto Ragionieri, for one, in his introduction to Togliatti's *Lezioni sul fascismo* (see supra, footnote 6), which analyzes in detail the complex and nuanced conception of fascism in Togliatti's writings – defined as a 'reactionary mass regime' – quotes approvingly a statement made by Lenin soon after the March on Rome where he equates fascism . . . with the Black Hundreds!

Poulantzas's Interpretation of Fascism

The main theses of Poulantzas on fascism may be summarized as follows:

1. Fascism belongs to the imperialist stage of capitalism. Imperialism is to be understood not as an exclusively economic phenomenon, but as a new articulation of the capitalist system as a whole which produces profound changes in politics and ideology (the appearance of the interventionist State – an intervention which is increased by the role the State plays in the transitional phases, with the formation of imperialist ideology). At the international level the key concepts are the *imperialist chain* and the unequal development of its links. Although a socialist revolution was made in the weakest link in the chain – Russia – fascism arose in the next two links.

2. The relative weakness of the links in the imperialist chain does not depend on a process of backwardness or the rhythm of economic development, but on an accumulation of contradictions. This accumulation was due, in Germany, to the rapid expansion and concentration of capital in a country where the bourgeois revolution was not carried out under the hegemony of the bourgeoisie, but of the Prussian Junkers. This permitted the survival of various handicaps such as the failure to complete the process of national unification, and the disproportionate political weight of the Junkers within the State apparatus relative to their economic influence. The outcome was that, when monopoly capital needed massive State intervention in its favour, the structure of the power bloc and the relative strength of the various non-monopoly groups within it was revealed as an obstacle. The process was even more accentuated in Italy where the power bloc comprising the industrialists of the North and the landowners of the Mezzogiorno, had established the hegemony of the former by maintaining the feudal character of agriculture in the South. This made it impossible to carry out a French-style agrarian reform. The maintenance of this anachronistic alliance was revealed as an insuperable obstacle during the phase of transition towards monopoly capitalism. This accumulation of contradictions

led to fascism in both countries. In England, the United States or France, where the same transition took place but where a similar accumulation of contradictions did not exist, fascism was not able to impose itself.

3. The rise and coming to power of fascism correspond to the deepening and sharpening of the internal contradictions between the dominant classes and class fractions. No class or class fraction was able to impose its leadership on the other classes and fractions of the power bloc, whether by its own methods of political organization or through the 'parliamentary democratic' State. Fascism corresponds to a reorganization of this bloc which imposes the hegemony of a new class fraction: big monopoly capital. This transition is effected through a political crisis – which implies the breaking of representational ties between classes and the political parties which represent them – and through a crisis of dominant ideology which develops into a generalized ideological crisis. The growth of fascism corresponds to an offensive strategy of the bourgeoisie and a defensive step for the workers' movement. In contrast to various conceptions in which fascism is the pure and simple dictatorship of monopoly capital, or a bonapartist regime based on an equilibrium of forces, or a political dictatorship of the petty-bourgeoisie, the fascist State has for Poulantzas a relative autonomy from both the power bloc and the fraction of big monopoly capital whose hegemony it has established. This relative autonomy stems from the internal contradictions of the classes and fractions in the power bloc as well as from the contradictions between dominant and dominated classes.

4. The beginning of the rise of fascism presupposes a significant number of working class defeats. During this process, the struggle of the bourgeoisie against the working class assumes an increasingly political character, while the working class struggle against the bourgeoisie falls further and further back into the domain of economic demands. The rise of fascism corresponds to a crisis of the revolutionary organizations and an ideological crisis of the working class. The crisis of the revolutionary organizations expresses itself in the emergence of internal divisions, and the severing of links between the

organizations and the masses. The ideological crisis takes the form of an increase in the influence of bourgeois ideology (trade unionism and reformism) and petty-bourgeois ideology (anarchism, spontaneism and 'putschist jaquerie'). A fundamental error recurs behind every tactical and strategic error of the working class: economism. Once in power fascism plays a dual role: organized physical repression of the working class on one hand, and ideological mobilization – using workerist ideology – on the other.

5. The petty-bourgeoise plays an essential role in the coming of fascism to power. Characteristic of the petty-bourgeoisie is that its unity as a class is expressed not at the level of economic relations but to the extent that the various economic insertions of its different fractions produce the same pertinent effects on the political and ideological levels. The petty-bourgeoisie is thus unified as a class on these two levels. Petty-bourgeois ideological discourse can only be that of one of the basic classes in capitalist society: the bourgeoisie or the working class; but there is a specific sub-ensemble of petty-bourgeois ideology which incorporates its own 'elements' into the dominant ideology. These elements are 'status quo anti-capitalism', the myth of the ladder and the fetishism of the State. The rise of fascism corresponds to an economic crisis for the petty-bourgeoisie. This determines a political crisis for it and the constitution of the petty-bourgeoisie into an authentic social force through the fascist parties. The historical role of fascism is to create an alliance between big monopoly capital and the petty-bourgeoisie. Finally, and this aspect is decisive, the rise of fascism corresponds to an acute ideological crisis of the petty-bourgeoisie, which has the following characteristics: petty-bourgeois elements become dissociated from dominant bourgeois discourse; the aspect of 'status quo anti-capitalism' becomes uppermost, by implicit opposition to bourgeois ideology; more and more ideological elements are taken from working-class ideology. The petty-bourgeois ideological sub-ensemble, modified in this way, 'replaces' the dominant bourgeois ideology, thereby cementing back together the social formation in question. This is the decisive element in the coming to power of fascism and is what distinguishes it from other

forms of exceptional State such as bonapartism and military dictatorship.

6. Poulantzas maintains that fascism is basically an urban phenomenon, in contrast to those tendencies which view it as a peasant-based movement. The role of rural fascism was clearly a subsidiary one, and where it developed, has comprised an ideological and military movement with direct ties to big property. Once in power, fascism favoured the expansion of monopoly capital in rural sectors, to the exclusive benefit of big property and the rich peasantry.

7. Finally, having demonstrated that the function of the fascist State has been to establish and organize the hegemony of monopoly capital, Poulantzas analyzes in detail the type of State and regime characterizing fascism, which he regards as a special case of the exceptional State.

As we can see, Poulantzas's analysis focusses on two aspects: the type of crisis from which fascism emerges and the form of State whereby that crisis is resolved. The crisis enables the petty-bourgeoisie to move to the uppermost plane of political life; and the crisis is resolved by the neutralization of the petty-bourgeoisie through a type of State which establishes the hegemony of monopoly capital. The petty-bourgeoisie plays, then, the central *political* role in the emergence of fascism. But in the class determination of the petty-bourgeoisie it is ideology which plays the decisive role ('the petty-bourgeoisie literally feeds on the ideology which cements it'). Consequently, the validity of Poulantzas's analysis as a whole rests on two fundamental components: his conception of ideology, and his conception of the petty-bourgeoisie. We will now proceed to some critical observations concerning both these aspects.

Ideological 'Elements' and their Class Belonging

Let us start with ideology. For Poulantzas fascism emerges from, among other things, an ideological crisis. In a crisis all the component elements and conditions fuse, as a whole, into a ruptural unity (Althusser). *Condensation* is the term used to define this process of fusion. The expression is an exact one to the extent that we accept it literally. In psychoanalysis – whence the term is derived – by condensation is understood the process by which 'A single representation represents in itself many associative chains at the intersection of which it is situated. From the economic point of view it is then invested with energies which, attached to those different chains, add to it . . .'. In the case of the interpretation of dreams, 'it is expressed by the fact that the manifest account is laconic in comparison with the latent content: it constitutes an abridged translation. Condensation should not, however, be likened to a resumé: if every manifest element is determined by various latent meanings, inversely each one of these can be found again in various elements: on the other hand, the manifest element does not represent in the same relation each of the meanings from which it derives, so that it does not subsume them in the way that a concept would do'.[21]

This means that the analysis of any crisis has a twin objective: 1. to analyze the constituent elements in the condensation; 2. to analyze the process of condensation itself. If we confine ourselves to the first task, we will be able to explain the *elements* and *conditions* of the crisis, but not the crisis itself. This is precisely what happens with Poulantzas: although his analysis captures all the complexity of the crisis from which fascism emerges – and thereby overcomes the errors mentioned earlier of those who reduce fascism to a simple contradiction – on the other hand, this complexity is presented on a merely descriptive level, by a simple adding together of the constitutive elements, without explaining how it became translated into a ruptural unity: that is to say, the process of its condensation. I think the reason for this lies in the limited and ambiguous conception of ideology revealed in Poulantzas's analysis of fascism.

What is this conception? In the first place, to analyze an ideology is, for Poulantzas, to break it down into its constitutive *elements* according to their belonging. Thus, dominant

[21] Jean Laplanche and J. B. Pontalis, *Vocabulaire de la Psychanalyse*, Paris, 1967.

bourgeois ideology contains petty-bourgeois *elements* which are incorporated in it, as well as working class elements. The collusion between petty-bourgeois ideology and imperialist ideology is explained by the existence of *elements* which are common to both (such as statolatry, nationalism, anti-semitic racism, militarism, anti-clericalism or elitism). Similarly, the elements common to 'transformed' feudal ideology and imperialist ideology (expansionist nationalism, militarism, the cult of despotism and of state authority) are those which would explain the weakness of liberalism in the Weimar Republic. In some cases these 'elements' are simply inchoate – as when reference is made to the 'seeds' of fascism encountered in Italian liberalism. This conception is combined with another which is complementary to it: social classes have 'pure', 'necessary' or 'paradigmatic' ideologies. In this sense Poulantzas is categorical. Thus Marxist-Leninist ideology is the ideology of the working class. Liberalism is bourgeois ideology in the stage of competitive capitalism, and if things happened differently in Germany it was because the capitalist mode of production was articulated with the feudal, and because national unification was carried out under the hegemony of Prussian Junkers (it is characteristic that, for Poulantzas, the absence of a strong German liberalism is the symbol and symptom of an incompleted bourgeois revolution). The mixture of nationalism, militarism, racism, and so on, forms imperialist ideology. As for the petty-bourgeoisie, since it is not one of the basic classes in social formations dominated by the capitalist mode of production, its ideology can only comprise 'elements' incorporated into the ideological discourse of the dominant class. We can see that the discrimination of 'elements' in terms of their class belonging, and the abstract postulation of pure ideologies, are mutually dependent aspects: only by implicit or explicit reference to those pure ideologies is it possible to analyze concrete historical ideologies by discriminating between their constitutive elements.

The second aspect characteristic of the Poulantzian conception of ideologies is, up to a point, a corollary of the first: concrete historical ideologies are an amalgam of heterogeneous elements (it being understood that for Poulantzas, each element has its class belonging). This criterion is systematically applied in the case of fascism. On several occasions Poulantzas quotes with approval the following assertions of Togliatti: 'Fascist ideology contains a series of heterogeneous elements . . . This serves to weld together several currents in the struggle for a dictatorship over the working masses and to create for this purpose a vast mass movement. Fascist ideology is an instrument created so as to keep these elements linked'.[22] At times Poulantzas carries this tendency to dissolve fascist ideological discourse into its component elements to such extremes as to simply deny its unity: fascism then has a distinct political discourse for each social sector. Thus, he has recently written: 'The role of fascist ideology among the popular masses was not at all one of a mere repetition of an identical discourse, via *propaganda techniques,* to atomized and undifferentiated masses . . . *On the contrary,* this role is due to the fact that these ideologies and discourses *present themselves in a considerably differentiated way, such that they are embodied in various fascist politico-ideological apparatuses, according to the various classes, class fractions and social categories to which they are addressed: and it is precisely this which enabled them to exploit the material conditions of existence of these classes and fractions* . . .'[23]

Finally, we must point out a third aspect relevant to our problem: that relating to the transformation of ideologies. Ideologies experience, for Poulantzas, a process of transformation. Thus, in referring to the adaptation of Prussian ideology to the requirements of a power bloc which has come to include the bourgeoisie, he speaks of a '*transformed*' feudal ideology. He also mentions, with regard to Italy, 'some kind of "continuous" *transmutation* of (the) "liberal nationalist" ideology into "imperialist fascist" ideology'. Elsewhere he speaks of the *metamorphosis* of nationalism. What this transformation consists of is never clearly formulated, although allusive expressions abound (transformation, transmutation, metamorphosis). But we should not be misled: for Poulantzas, 'transmutation' never means that the characteristic elements of an ideology change their class belonging, such that, for example,

[22] Palmiro Togliatti, *Lezioni sul Fascismo,* Rome, 1970, p. 15.

[23] Nicos Poulantzas, 'A propos de l'impact populaire du fascisme', in Maria A. Macciocchi, *Elements pour une analyse du fascisme,* Paris, 1976.

'transformed' feudal ideology become bourgeois ideology. The transformation consists in the incorporation of bourgeois 'elements' into an ideology which *in its essential elements* continues to be feudal (if not, the absence of a liberal tradition would not seem to him to be an index of the hegemonic weakness of the German bourgeoisie).[24] In the event of the transformation affecting the class belonging of the very 'elements' of ideology – such as the take-over of transformed feudal ideology by imperialist ideology – Poulantzas has his response ready: this is possible because the essential elements of 'transformed' feudal ideology – authoritarianism or militarism – coincide with the essential elements of imperialist ideology. Two transformations have taken place – the incorporation of bourgeois elements into feudal ideology, and the take-over of essential elements of it by imperialist ideology – without the theory of class belonging of ideological 'elements' having to be modified one iota. In the Italian case, where the offensive of imperialist capital took place in a contrary manner, that is to say, by appropriating the nationalist liberal traditions of the Risorgimento, and where therefore one cannot say that the essential elements of the ideologies coincide, Poulantzas resolves the problem by saying that it was a question of demagogic fraud: 'This ideological offensive was a covert one, in that it was masked by the direct monopolization of certain aspects of liberal-nationalist ideology, the ideology of Italian medium capital'.[25]

By means of these various expedients, therefore, the class belonging of ideological elements remains intact. It is no surprise then, when Poulantzas discusses the political strategies of the Comintern, that he tends to consider any kind of nationalist agitation as a concession to the adversary. Thus, in his discussion of the Schlageter line – whereby Radek proposed to initiate nationalist agitation in Germany against the Versailles Treaty – Poulantzas considers it inadmissible opportunism. He states: 'The key factor . . . is that the chauvinist turn *produced no reaction in the Comintern Plenum.* The

[24] I am not trying to deny the specific weaknesses of the German bourgeoisie, but simply that the inadequate development of liberalism can be regarded as a *necessary* index of these weaknesses.

[25] N. Poulantzas, *Fascism . . ., op. cit.*, p. 128.

view was even expressed that the agitation against the treaty had not been sufficiently exploited. Lenin, of course, had described this treaty as the "most monstrous act of piracy" in history, but he *never lent his authority* to a social-chauvinist use of the question'.[26] If, despite it being an 'act of piracy', it was not possible to agitate against the Versailles Treaty because this would have been chauvinist, this is because for Poulantzas nationalism is an 'element' of bourgeois ideology and, as such, is not susceptible to transformation in a socialist direction. A socialist nationalism would, in this view, be a perfectly contradictory expression.[27]

Class determination of ideological elements, concrete ideologies as an amalgam of elements, transformation of ideologies through an incorporation/articulation of ideological class elements – what criticisms does this approach merit? In the first place, the process of pronouncing the class belonging of elements of concrete ideologies is a purely arbitrary one; as we shall see, it not only fails to theoretically construct its object but, on the contrary, *presupposes* empirical knowledge of it, and operates taxonomically on that knowledge. In fact, none of the elements or aspects that Poulantzas supposes to be characteristics of the ideology of any one class is such if considered in isolation. Liberalism, which Poulantzas considers an ideological 'element' of the bourgeoisie during the stage of

[26] *Ibid.*, p. 170.

[27] In a recent book Poulantzas seems to present a more developed position in this respect. He states: 'The ambiguities and metamorphoses of nationalism are very familiar: in the imperialist stage this has gradually come to take a highly reactionary aspect in the dominant countries, while in the dominated countries by way of their demands for "national liberation" it has assumed a progressive aspect. What we are concerned with here is particularly the nationalism of the present phase of imperialism, as this affects the European countries in general, and those we are dealing with here in particular. To put it rather summarily, the new dependence of the European countries vis-à-vis the dominant imperialism of the United States means that nationalism can now again have a certain progressive character in these countries, even though they do not belong to the traditional zone of the Third World or the 'under-developed' countries, but actually form part of the dominant sphere; this was the case with certain progressive aspects of Gaullist nationalism in France.' *The Crisis of the Dictatorships*, NLB, 1976, p. 114. This paragraph, however, is too ambiguous for us to conclude that Poulantzas's position has changed: it could be interpreted in the sense that nationalism has ceased to be a bourgeois ideological element, but also in the sense that it is an ideological element of certain relatively more progressive sectors of the bourgeoisie..

competitive capitalism was, in Latin America, the characteristic ideology of the feudal landowners. Militarism is not necessarily an imperialist or feudal ideology: in 19th century Spain, military 'pronouncements' were the typical expression of incipient bourgeois sectors, and after the Second World War, militarism throughout the Third World was often an essential ideological ingredient of anti-imperialist and anti-feudal movements. The same could be said of nationalism, of 'statolatry', authoritarianism, and in fact *all* the ideological elements to which Poulantzas assigns a class belonging. Even antisemitism can be an ideological trait characteristic of the most divergent classes: in Eastern Europe during the 19th century it was a frequent ideological component of the liberal bourgeoisie because of the support lent by sectors of Hebrew usurious capital to the multinational Tsarist, Austro-Hungarian and Turkish empires;[28] and during the Middle Ages it was even on occasion an element of the ideologies of popular sectors, because of the exploitative role played by usurious capital in the interstices of feudal society.[29] What conclusions can be drawn from these observations? That we are confronted with

[28] At the base of this support was the indissoluble link between usury capital and feudal society. According to Abraham Leon: 'The accumulation of money in the hands of the Jews did not result from a special form of production, capitalist production. Surplus value (or surplus produce) resulted from feudal exploitation and the feudal Lords were obliged to leave a part of this surplus value to the Jews. It is from here that the antagonism between the Jews and Feudalism arises, but it is also from here that stems the indissoluble link which existed between them'. (*La Conception Materialiste de la Question Juive,* Paris, 1968, p. 25.) Thereby the development of capitalism had to enter quickly in conflict with usury capital. As Leon says, referring to 15th century Poland: 'The backward state of the country had also hindered the evolution which we have observed in Eastern European countries: the eviction of Jews from commercial activities and their confinement to usury. The bourgeois class and the cities were at that time only beginning to develop. The struggle of the bourgeoisie against the Jews was at an embryonic state and did not lead to decisive results. The artisans, also suffering from the Jewish usury, joined the merchants. Here too, as soon as a province developed, the conflicts with the Jews arose. In 1403, in Cracow, and in 1445 in Boehnie, the artisans provoked the massacres of Jews. . . . '

[29] We quote Leon once again: 'As usury became the main occupation of the Jews, they gradually became more in contact with the popular masses and these realtionships worsened continuously. It was not the need for luxury which pushed the peasant or the artisan to borrow from the Jewish usurer but the blackest distress. They pawned the working tools which often were indispensable to ensure their subsistence. One can understand the hatred that the

cases whose divergence from 'paradigmatic' ideologies is explained by an overdetermination of contradictions whose interpretation constitutes the scientific analysis of ideologies? This method, inspired by the metaphysical assignment to classes of certain ideological 'elements' can only lead to a multiplication ad infinitum of increasingly formal distinctions. I think the correct method is the reverse: *to accept that ideological 'elements' taken in isolation have no necessary class connotation, and that this connotation is only the result of the articulation of those elements in a concrete ideological discourse. This means that the precondition for analyzing the class nature of an ideology is to conduct the inquiry through that which constitutes the distinctive unity of an ideological discourse.*

Poulantzas, however, proceeds to evoke or allude to this unity as the basis of his whole analysis. For what is the actual proof that ideological elements have a precise class connotation? In speaking of militarism, authoritarianism, etc., Poulantzas does not theoretically construct these concepts but *evokes* them before the mind of the reader, who, because of his empirical knowledge of the unified discourse of which these elements form a part, tends to assign to them the class nature of that discourse. Further, the isolated 'elements' will be considered as symbols of the ideologies in question and of their class connotation. Consequently, not only is the concrete – the unity of the ideology in question – not theoretically constructed, but the syncretic intuition of that unity, at the level of the raw material of knowledge, forms the only basis for judging the class connotations of the isolated elements. From this derives the basic inadequacy of this study of fascism which we mentioned earlier: the elements are presented in all their complexity – and it has to be said that Poulantzas does not minimize any of the complexities of the fascist phenomenon – but the unity in which these complexities are resolved is presupposed and

common man must have felt towards the Jew whom he saw as the direct cause of his ruin without perceiving the Emperor, the Prince or the rich Bourgeois – all of whom grew wealthier thanks to Jewish usury. It was mainly in Germany that the latter took its most 'popular' form, principally in the 14th and 15th centuries, when hatred against the Jews was more evident, hatred whose outcome were the anti-Jew massacres and the 'burning' of Jews (judenbrand)' (*op. cit.*, pp. 102–3).

not explained. That is to say, *the condensation of contradictions comprizing the crisis cannot be fully understood.* We remain lost in a taxonomical labyrinth, without knowing exactly in what consists the peculiar fusion of contradictions from which fascism emerges.

If we want to get out of this impasse, we must try and answer two essential questions: what comprises the unity of an ideological discourse and what is the process of transformation of ideologies? The answer to these two questions takes us to the very centre of the problems which a Marxist theory of fascism must tackle.

Class Interpellations and Popular-democratic Interpellations

It is strange that Poulantzas, who operates within the general framework of the Althusserian problematic, has not retained Althusser's most important and specific contribution to the study of ideologies: the conception that the basic function of all ideology is to interpellate/constitute individuals as subjects. According to Althusser – who in this instance is strongly influenced by the conception of Lacan in which the 'mirror-phase' plays a decisive role in the formation and moulding of the self, 'The category of the subject is constitutive of all ideology, but at the same time and immediately I add that the category of subject is only constitutive of all ideology insofar as all ideology has the function (which defines it) of "constituting" concrete individuals as subjects'.[30] *Individuals,* who are simple bearers of structures, are transformed by ideology into *subjects,* that is to say, that they live the relation with their real conditions of existence as if they themselves were the *autonomous principle* of determination of that relation. The mechanism of this characteristic inversion is interpellation.

Althusser writes: 'Ideology "acts" or "functions" in such a way that it "recruits" subjects among the individuals (it recruits them all), or "transforms" the individuals into subjects (it transforms them all) by the very precise operation that

[30] Louis Althusser, *Lenin and Philosophy and Other Essays,* London, 1971, p. 160.

I have called interpellation or hailing, and which can be imagined along the lines of the most common everyday police (or other) hailing: "Hey, you there!" . . .'[31] If, therefore, the basic function of all ideology is to constitute individuals as subjects, and if through interpellation individuals live their conditions of existence as if they were the autonomous principle of the latter – as if they, the determinate, constituted the determinant – it is clear that the unity of the distinct aspects of an ideological system is given by the specific interpellation which forms the axis and organizing principle of all ideology. Who is the interpellated subject? This is the key question in the analysis of ideologies. We can now answer our first question: *what constitutes the unifying principle of an ideological discourse is the 'subject' interpellated and thus constituted through this discourse.*[32] The isolated elements of a discourse

[31] *Ibid.*, p. 162.

[32] We must point out, if only briefly, that the Althusserian conception of ideology still presents serious difficulties. In the first place, the mechanism of interpellation not only has for Althusser the function of transforming in an imaginary way the individual into a subject, but also of carrying out his self-subjection to the dominant system, and thus ensuring social reproduction as a whole. In this sense, it has been pointed out, any ideology must be a dominant ideology and there is no possibility of the existence of an ideology of dominated sectors. Secondly, ideology is, for Althusser, *simultaneously* a level of any social formation and the opposite of science, which creates serious theoretical difficulties. We cannot here go into the theoretical debate about these problems which has recently taken place, in any detail (cf. Jacques Rancière, *La leçon d'Althusser*, Paris, 1974 and Emilio de Ipola, 'Critica a la teoria de Althusser sobre la ideologia', *Uno en Dos*, Medellin (Colombia), July 1975, pp. 7–39). For the purposes of this essay, it is sufficient to make the following points: (1) class struggle enters the arena of ideology in such a manner that we find, together with ideologies of the dominant classes which tend to the reproduction of the system, also ideologies of the dominated sectors which tend towards their revolutionary transformation; (2) that if the mechanism of self-subjection of the individual functions in the ideologies of the dominant sectors to ensure the existing system of domination, in the ideologies of dominated classes the same mechanism functions to link individuals to their task of opposition to that system. The ethical compulsion is thus an abstract mechanism which can respond to the most varied of objective interests; (3) that the mechanism of interpellation as constitutive of ideology operates in the same way in ideologies of dominant classes and in revolutionary ideologies. As de Ipola points out: 'A juridical (and rhetorical) figure, interpellation may be detected both in a Christian religious discourse and in humanist discourse, and even in communist discourse such as that of the Communist Manifesto ("Workers of all countries unite!"). In some cases, interpellation of "subjects" will be the concealed form of effectively ensuring a subjection; in others, by contrast, as in the Communist Manifesto, it will take the form of a political slogan which

have no meaning in themselves. In trying to analyze the ideological level of a determinate social formation, our first task must be to reconstruct the interpellative structures which constitute it. It is in this sense surprising that Poulantzas, who devotes so much attention to the ideological crisis from which fascism emerged, devotes not a single line to the problem of the characteristic interpellations of fascist ideologies.

There are different types of interpellations (political, religious, familial, etc.) which coexist whilst being articulated within an ideological discourse in a relative unity. Strictly speaking, each one of the 'elements' or 'aspects' discussed by Poulantzas, implies interpellations. In what way is one interpellation articulated with another, that is to say, what is it that enables them both to form part of a relatively unified ideological discourse? By unity we must not necessarily understand logical consistency – on the contrary, the ideological unity of a discourse is perfectly compatible with a wide margin of logical inconsistency – but the ability of each interpellative element to fulfill a role of condensation which respect to the others. When a familial interpellation, for example, *evokes* a political interpellation, a religious interpellation, or an aesthetic interpellation, and when each of these isolated interpellations operates as a *symbol* of the others, we have a relatively unified ideological discourse. Various efforts can be made to rationalize this unity in an explicit way, but they are always *a posteriori* attempts, which operate on the initial basis of an *implicit* unity of ideological discourse. In this regard we can point out a basic difference between two types of situations. In periods of stability, when the social formation tends to reproduce its relations following traditional channels and succeeds in neutralizing its contradictions by *displacements*,[33] this is when the dominant bloc in the formation is able to absorb most of the contradictions and its ideological discourse tends to rest more on the purely implicit mechanisms of its

calls for the creation of conditions for the emancipation of the exploited' (*op. cit.*, p. 38).

[33] 'In periods of stability the essential contradictions of the social formation are neutralized by displacement; in a revolutionary situation, however, they may condense or fuse into a revolutionary rupture.' (Ben Brewster, 'Glossary' to Louis Althusser, *For Marx*, London, NLB, 1977.)

unity. This is when, generally, the correlation between the logical consistency of the elements of the discourse and its ideological unity reaches its lowest point. (Religious interpellations of an ascetic type can, for example, coexist with an increasing enjoyment of worldly goods without the social agents 'living' them as incompatible.)

In a period of generalized ideological crisis such as Poulantzas locates at the origin of fascism, the opposite tends to occur. The crisis of confidence in the 'natural' or 'automatic' reproduction of the system is translated into an exacerbation of all the ideological contradictions and into a dissolution of the unity of the dominant ideological discourse. As the function of all ideology is to constitute individuals as subjects, this ideological crisis is necessarily translated into an 'identity crisis' of the social agents. Each one of the sectors in struggle will try and reconstitute a new ideological unity using a 'system of narration'[34] as a vehicle which disarticulates the ideological discourses of the opposing forces. What is important for the present problem is that one of the possible ways of resolving the crisis for the new hegemonic class or fraction is to deny all interpellations but one, develop all the logical implications of this one interpellation and transform it into a critique of the existing system, and at the same time, into a principle of reconstruction of the entire ideological domain. In our previous example, the incompatibility between religious asceticism and enjoyment of material wealth, formerly masked by the dominant ideological discourse, erupts in all its sharpness during a crisis period. There arises in these circumstances a religious reformer who blames all the evils on corruption and the abandonment of strict ascetic observance and who,

[34] In the sense used by Jean-Pierre Faye in his excellent book *Langages Totalitaires*, Paris, 1972. 'Each class of the population therefore possessed its *system* of narration. . . . The struggle of narrative versions bears in itself – or refers to – the formidable weight of what is at stake. To narrate the action is not just to "write together" – as Thucydides would have it: *syn-graphien*; the different witnesses who are also actors (or acting), change their action by the differences being narrated. The way in which the double process of the *narrated event* and the *narrative propositions* takes one into a generalized economy where the whole of history, and not only "economic history" is caught and enveloped, is what has to be shown, thinking of that science of history of which Marx has written . . . that it embraces all sciences.' J. P. Faye, *Théorie du recit*, Paris, 1972, pp. 16, 39.

through his interpellation, gives his followers a new subjectivity. The religious interpellation thus comes to be a chief reorganizer of all familial, political, economic, and other aspects. The coexistence of various relatively consistent interpellations in an ideological discourse has given way to an ideological structure in which *one* interpellation becomes the main organizer of all the others. In our example religious ideology fulfills this central role, but, in other historical contexts it could be political ideology. Whether the crisis is resolved in this way depends on many historical circumstances, but we can indicate at least two which would favour this type of solution: (1) the more separated is a social sector from the dominant relations of production, and the more diffuse are its 'objective interests' and consequently, less developed its 'class instinct' – the more the evolution and the resolution of the crisis will tend to take place on the ideological level; (2) the more central is the role of this type of sector in the social formation in question, the more central will be the role of the ideological level in the final resolution of the crisis on the part of the social formation as a whole. We will see the importance of these observations for the analysis of fascism.

We have omitted a central issue from our previous discussion: the relation between ideologies and the class struggle. This is, however, a fundamental problem if we want to answer our second question: how are ideologies transformed? It must be pointed out in this respect that there has existed a basic ambiguity within the Marxist tradition about the use of the concept *class struggle*. In one sense, class struggle is posed at the level of the mode of production: the production relation which constitutes its two poles as classes is an antagonistic relation. Surplus-value, for example, constitutes *simultaneously* the relation between capitalists and workers and the antagonism between them; or rather, it constitutes that relation as an antagonistic one. Two conclusions follow from this: (1) that there are no classes except in a relation of struggle; (2) that the level of analysis which makes this antagonism intelligible is that of the mode of production. But the concept of class struggle has also tended to be applied to another kind of antagonism: to that where the struggle between classes only becomes intelligible if the overall political and ideological relations of domination characterizing a determinate social formation are brought to bear. Let us take, for example, the case of a social formation in which there is an articulation between a capitalist and a feudal mode of production and where a feudal landowning class is the hegemonic class in the dominant power bloc. It is not just the peasants who are exploited (those whom the hegemonic fraction exploits directly at the level of the mode of production), but the dominated sectors as a whole – petty-bourgeoisie, urban workers, perhaps part of the bourgeoisie, etc. Classes are, in this case, also *in struggle*, but can we speak strictly of a *class struggle*? This type of antagonism is distinct from the first in two basic senses: (1) unlike the first, it does not constitute classes as such (we cannot think of the concept of worker without thinking of the correlative concept of capitalist, but we can think of the concept of capitalist without thinking of the concept petty-bourgeois); (2) whilst the first antagonism is intelligible at the abstract level of the mode of production, the second antagonism is only intelligible at the level of a concrete social formation. The problem which then arises is: what is the relation between these two kinds of antagonism? Closely linked to the previous question is another: what is the relation between the ideologies in which both kinds of antagonism are expressed?

This presents no problem for a traditional Marxist conception: all ideological content has a clear class connotation and any contradiction can be reduced – through a more or less complicated system of mediations – to a class contradiction. The two kinds of antagonism are not articulated: in fact the second can be reduced to the first. In the paradigmatic case, the bourgeoisie exploits the working class at the level of the mode of production and constitutes the dominant class at the level of the social formation. Here the two kinds of struggle coincide and the only relevant distinction is the traditional one between *economic struggle* and *political* struggle. If, on the contrary, we have a situation as in our previous example where the power bloc is in opposition to the petty-bourgeoisie, the peasantry, the working class and certain sectors of the bourgeoisie, the picture becomes more complex but is not essentially modified: one would conclude that those sectors must establish a 'class alliance' to which each one must join within its own ideology, its own interests and, if possible, with its own party[35] in the struggle against the common enemy. If this struggle created a series of ideological contents – values, symbols, etc., in short specific popular democratic interpellations which went beyond the ideologies of the different forces comprising the pact – this would be rejected as an element of rhetoric, propaganda, etc.; and anyone insisting on the autonomy of this aspect would be dismissed as 'idealist'. If, within this perspective, the priority of certain 'democratic' tasks is asserted, this is because there are some bourgeois tasks yet to be fulfilled: this is where 'combined and unequal development' is summoned to explain the more complex combinations and alliances, which never call into question the reduction of all contradictions to class contradictions.

To this reductionist approach we counterpose the following thesis: (1) Class struggle is only that which constitutes classes as such; (2) Consequently, not every contradiction is a class contradiction, but every contradiction is overdetermined by the class struggle. Let us start with the first thesis. Its obvious consequence is that the second type of antagonism cannot, strictly speaking, be regarded as a class struggle. Note that it is not possible to evade the problem by stating, in our previous example, that the petty-bourgeoisie is one class, the feudal landowners another and that therefore the conflict between them is a class struggle. This is the way in which the class struggle is typically presented in bourgeois literature of social history. But, in the first place, classes appear *already* constituted and the confrontation is relatively external to their nature; this has little to do with the Marxist conception of classes according to which they constitute themselves through the act of struggle itself. Secondly, even if there are two classes confronting each other, in the conflict mentioned, it is obvious that they are not in confrontation *as classes*, that their class nature – their insertion in the production process – is relatively

[35] This type of approach, which characterized to a great extent the frontist strategies of the Comintern after 1935, is what explains a feature of Comintern policy to which Poulantzas has sharply called attention: the Comintern assigned little importance to mass action of communists within the peasantry and the petty-bourgeoisie. Those sectors 'must *firstly and mainly* be drawn in through their "own parties", which if they did not exist would have to be invented'. (Poulantzas, *Fascism . . ., op. cit.*, p. 165.)

external to the confrontation itself. We have *classes in struggle*, but not *class struggle*.

Consequently, if this antagonism is not a class antagonism, the ideologies which express it cannot be class ideologies. Through this kind of antagonism, the dominated sectors would not identify themselves as a class but as 'the other', 'the counterposed' to the dominant power bloc, as the *underdog*. If the first contradiction – at the level of mode of production – is expressed on the ideological level in the interpellation of the agents as a *class*, this second contradiction is expressed through the interpellation of the agents as *the people*. The first contradiction is the sphere of *class struggle*; the second, that of *popular-democratic struggle*.[36] The 'people' or 'popular sectors'

[36] Let us clarify two points to prevent any misunderstanding. Firstly, not every non-class interpellation is a popular democratic interpellation (otherwise the latter would be a purely residual category). To be able to speak of a popular-democratic interpellation, the subject addressed as 'the people' must be so in terms of an antagonistic relationship regarding the dominant bloc. Secondly, by democracy we do not mean anything which has a necessary relationship with Liberal parliamentary institutions. (The popular-democratic ideologies in the countries of the Third World have frequently been expressed in nationalist and anti-imperialist forms which led, once the process of decolonization was over, to military regimes.) Thus by democracy we understand *something more* than quite straightforward measures establishing civil freedom, equality and self-government for the masses of the people. This purely negative conception of democracy stems directly from liberal philosophy which, in reducing social agents to the juridical vacuity of the 'citizen', was impeded from legislating any further than certain abstract forms of participation that the juridical system guarantees to every individual. This conception has frequently been accompanied in Marxism – though not always – by 'revolutionary cynicism': i.e. by the idea that the working class must simply 'utilize' the existing democratic framework for its political activities, propaganda, etc., until the moment comes when it will be strong enough to impose a dictatorship of the proletariat. In the sense it has been given in this text, by democracy we understand a set of symbols, values, etc. – in short, interpellations – through which the 'people' grows aware of its identity through its confrontation with the power bloc. These interpellations are necessarily united to institutions in which democracy is materialized, but both aspects are indissoluble. One cannot conceive an extension of democratic rights without the parallel production of the subjects capable of exercising them. In this sense, our conception of democracy must be differentiated both from Liberalism and from 'revolutionary cynicism'. The former hypostasizes an abstract condition – citizenship – and transforms it into the subject of a democracy conceived as a simple system of formal rights to participate in the decision-making processes. Herein the often remarked confluence between formal juridical equality and real exploitation. On the one hand, 'revolutionary cynicism' takes the subject 'working class' as having been constituted previously to its participation in democratic institutions and in a simple pragmatic relationship of utilization of

are not, as some conceptions suppose, rhetorical abstractions or a liberal or idealist conception smuggled into Marxist political discourse. The 'people' form an objective determination of the system which is different from the class determination: the people are one of the poles of the dominant contradiction in a social formation, that is, a contradiction whose intelligibility depends on the ensemble of political and ideological relations of domination and not just the relations of production. If class contradiction is the dominant contradiction at the abstract level of the mode of production, the people/power bloc contradiction is dominant at the level of the social formation. We must ask ourselves, then, what is the relation between these two contradictions, and as part of the same problem, what is the relation between class interpellation (=ideology) and popular-democratic interpellation (=ideology).

This enables us to return to our second thesis: if not every contradiction can be reduced to a class contradiction, every contradiction is overdetermined by class struggle. According to basic Marxist theory, the level of production relations always maintains the role of determination in the last instance in any social formation. This in itself establishes the priority of the class struggle over the popular-democratic struggle, since the latter takes place only at the ideological and political level (the 'people' do not, obviously, exist at the level of production relations). This priority is revealed in the fact that popular-democratic ideologies never present themselves separated from, but articulated with, class ideological discourses. Class struggle at the ideological level consists, to a great extent, in the attempt to articulate popular-democratic interpellations in the ideological discourses of antagonistic classes. *The popular-democratic interpellation not only has no precise*

---

them. On the contrary, in our conception, the real extension of the exercise of democracy and the production of popular subjects who are increasingly hegemonic, form two aspects of the same process. The advance towards a real democracy is a long march which will only be completed with the elimination of class exploitation. But this elimination must run parallel with the rejection of such exploitation by the immense majority of the population, i.e., by the creation of a historic subject in which both Socialism and Democracy would be condensed. The alternative to this process can only lie in the bureaucratic 'socialist' regimes of Eastern Europe.

class content, but is the domain of ideological class struggle par excellence. Every class struggles at the ideological level *simultaneously* as class and as the people, or rather, tries to give coherence to its ideological discourse by presenting its class objectives as the consummation of popular objectives.

The overdetermination of non-class interpellations by the class struggle consists, then, in the integration of those interpellations into a class ideological discourse. Since ideology is a practice producing subjects, this integration is the interpellation of a subject in whom partial interpellations are condensed. But as classes struggle to integrate the same interpellations into antagonistic ideological discourses, the process of condensation will never be complete: it will always have an ambiguity, a greater or lesser degree of openness according to the level of the class struggle, and various antagonistic attempts at fusion will always coexist. We are now in a position to answer our second question: how are ideologies transformed? The answer is: *through class struggle, which is carried out through the production of subjects and the articulation/disarticulation of discourses.*

I think it is now clear why Poulantzas's conception that Marxist-Leninist ideology is the ideology of the working class seems to me to be inadequate. Marxism-Leninism is at most one element in working class ideology. But the working class is also part of the 'people' – whose characteristics will depend on the social formation in question – and it will, therefore respond to a popular-democratic interpellation. The ideological discourse of the working class will be the condensation of both in a new subject. The ideological subject 'German working class', or 'Italian', 'English' etc., has then, an irreducible specificity because it is the condensation of a multiplicity of interpellations which cannot be reduced abstractly to Marxism-Leninism. The inadequacy of Poulantzas's analysis lies, in this respect, in the fact that he has ignored the autonomous domain of the popular-democratic struggle and has tried to find a class belonging in every ideological element.[37] To this

[37] I have frequently encountered the following objections: (1) when it is said that the Marxist-Leninist ideology is the ideology of the proletariat, the claim does not mean that all proletariats are Marxist-Leninist but that Marxist-Leninist ideology is the one that most adequately corresponds to the

extent he has had to conclude that concrete ideologies are an amalgam of elements. In the perspective we are suggesting, on the contrary, *although the domain of class determination is reduced, the arena of class struggle is immensely broadened, since it opens the possibility of integrating into a revolutionary and socialist ideological discourse, a multitude of elements and interpellations which have up to now appeared constitutive of bourgeois ideological discourse.* Not the least of the bourgeoisie's successes in asserting its ideological hegemony, is the consen-

---

class interest of the proletariat; (2) many other ideologies can flourish in the proletariat, but when they do they constitute a barrier to the achievement of its objective class interests. The first statement tries to establish a contraposition amongst empirically existing ideologies and ideologies corresponding to objective class interests. The second statement expresses the belief that this 'empirical' diversification constitutes a loss of purity for the Marxist-Leninist ideology, which is thereby degraded by the inclusion of foreign elements. The diversity of the subjects 'English working class', 'German working class', etc., would therefore consist of the subsistence of national and cultural lags which would have to be eliminated by the development of the proletarian 'class consciousness'. That is to say that the working class *would have nothing to win* from these incorporations. But this objection misses the essential part of our argument, which is that *from the point of view of its class interests,* the ideology of the proletariat can only consist of the articulation of Marxist-Leninist ideology to popular-democratic interpellations characteristic of a specific social formation. It is only through this type of articulation that the ideology of a class can present itself as a *hegemonic* ideology. This does not mean to say that *any* articulation is necessarily correct: there are many possibilities of articulation and the subjects created through them will be obviously different. But what constitutes an insufficient or erroneous articulation from the point of view of the interests of a dominated class, must be specified: an example would be acceptance as a matter of fact of the fusion between democratic interpellations and the ideology of the dominant class and a juxtaposition to the latter, as a merely corporative ideology, of one's own class interpellations. As we shall see, this is the case of the Social-Democracy.

Marxist-Leninist ideology is not, therefore, *the* ideology of the working class – let us state this clearly: it is not the ideology which responds to the class interests of the working class – but just one of its abstract and necessary conditions. Quite the contrary, to consider that Marxism-Leninism is already the *final form* of a wholly constituted working class ideology; to substitute, as a consequence, the concrete by one of its abstract conditions, is the ideological root of *ultra-leftism.* To the latter, the working class does not have a hegemonic function – disarticulation of bourgeois ideology and articulation of its democratic elements to working class ideology – since any non-class interpellation is by definition, within this perspective an alien and opposed element. At best, democratic elements must be used, but not fused into one's own ideology. The working class must not, therefore, *transform* bourgeois society but should *blow it up* and substitute it by another one which would come out of the minds of revolutionaries and would do so wholly constituted, as Minerva did from Jupiter's head. For the ultra-left, concrete struggles do not create 'correct' ideologies but merely help to mature consciousnesses until the latter accept sus it has achieved – shared by many revolutionaries – that many of the constitutive elements of democratic and popular culture in a country are irrevocably linked to its class ideology. That this is not the case, that popular-democratic interpellations have no precise class connotation and can be incorporated into quite distinct political discourses, is something of which fascism provides eloquent proof. For the thesis we wish to present is the following: that fascism, far from being the typical ideological expression of the most conservative and reactionary sectors of the dominant classes was, on the contrary, one of the possible ways of articulating the popular-democratic interpellations into political discourse. But before considering this point, we have to deal with a final theoretical problem: Poulantzas's conception of the petty-bourgeoisie.

The Class Nature of the Petty-bourgeoisie

When referring to the petty-bourgeoisie, Poulantzas tries to overcome the vagueness and imprecision with which concepts such as 'middle classes', 'middle sectors', etc., have been used in sociological literature, and which have even been incorporated into Marxist analysis. In this latter respect, his critique centres specifically about the French Communist Party's conception of these sectors. Thus he states: 'The PCF argument, while it rejects the dissolution of the wage-earning groupings into the working class, still denies their class specificity, or even their membership of a class as such. (They are in fact

---

without ambiguities or 'impurities' a truth pre-existent to the struggles themselves. As Hoederer says in Sartre's *Les mains sales*: 'You, I know you well my boy, you are a destroyer. Mankind, you detest because you detest yourself; your purity is like death and the Revolution of which you dream is not ours: you do not want to change the world, you want to blow it up.' (We will not discuss here whether Marxism-Leninism can be considered an ideology, an issue which would lead us to the core of the distinction between science and ideology. Let us merely remark that, whatever the position taken in that discussion, Marxism-Leninism has in any case *also* functioned as an ideology, as far as it has constituted a system of specific interpellations directed to a particular type of militant: the Communist militant. It is in this sense that we establish the distinction between *Marxism-Leninism* and *Marxist-Leninist* ideology. I think, moreover, that Poulantzas has in mind this kind of distinction when he refers to the deformation that Marxist-Leninist ideology can suffer as a result of the bourgeois and petty-bourgeois ideological influences.)

termed "*intermediate wage-earing strata*") . . . Nowhere does the *Traité* answer the question: What classes are these groupings strata of, what exactly is their class membership?'[38] This approach, in which intermediate sectors – whose class belonging is imprecise – will be polarized by the struggle between the two basic classes in the dominant mode of production, is regarded by Poulantzas as incorrect. 'The class struggle and the polarization it involves does not and cannot give rise to groupings alongside of or marginal to classes, groupings without class membership, for the simple reason that this class membership is itself nothing more than the class struggle, and that this struggle only exists by way of the existence of the places of social classes. Strictly speaking, it actually makes no sense to maintain that there are "social groupings" that are nevertheless involved in the class struggle.'[39]

Poulantzas consequently tries to determine the class nature of these 'intermediate layers', and he presents them as divided into two groups: the old and the new petty-bourgeoisie. The problem is that these groups act in a relatively unified way from the political and ideological point of view, but from the economic point of view they occupy clearly different places in the production process. How can their class unity be made compatible with the Marxist conception that economic relations are the basic criterion for the determination of classes? Poulantzas's answer is that politics and ideology also intervene in the class determination and that therefore the class unity of the petty-bourgeoisie is provided by the fact that distinct *places* in economic relations produce the same effects on the level of ideological and political relations.

Poulantzas has tried to cope with a real problem, but the solution he offers is clearly inadequate. He goes from saying that economic relations cannot be the *only* criterion in class determination, to excluding them *totally* from his definition of the class unity of the petty-bourgeoisie. Furthermore, the petty-bourgeoisie does not have, for Poulantzas, its own ideological discourse – and this is correct – rather its ideology

[38] N. Poulantzas, *Classes in Contemporary Capitalism,* London, NLB, 1975, p. 198. The sentence in parenthesis appears in the French edition but not in the English translation.

[39] *Ibid.,* p. 201.

consists in the incorporation of its own 'elements' into the ideological discourse of the basic classes in a capitalist social formation; it therefore has to be concluded, by *reductio ad absurdum*, that there belong to the petty-bourgeoisie those groups which incorporate status quo anti-capitalism, the myth of the ladder and statolatry into bourgeois political discourse. This does not seem much more convincing than the conceptions of 'middle sectors' that Poulantzas criticizes, but is on the contrary even more vague and imprecise. In addition, Poulantzas does not apply his criterion consistently: if in the case of the petty-bourgeoisie he carries to extremes the exclusion of economic relations from his conception of class, when he tries to determine the limits of the working class he embarks upon a long disquisition about productive and unproductive labour from which he concludes that only productive workers can be considered as members of the working class. He does not ask himself in this case whether the location of certain unproductive wage-earning sectors in economic relations could not produce *similar effects* at the level of political and ideological relations, enabling them to be considered as members of the working class.

It is not very difficult to discover the reason for the inadequacy of Poulantzas's analysis. Although he correctly poses the terms of the problem, and perceives *where* the solution is to be found, he is unable to formulate a satisfactory answer because he tries to do so within the general assumption that dominates his whole analysis: the reduction of every contradiction to a class contradiction, and the assignment of a class belonging to every ideological element. Starting from these assumptions, it is obvious that the relative ideological unity of the petty-bourgeoisie could alone signify its class unity, but this assertion leads, with an implacable logic, to a denial of the very bases of Marxism: that is, to a definition of class apart from production relations. Poulantzas says that the class characterization of the petty-bourgeoisie is the key point in the Marxist theory of social classes, and he is right. His analysis proves that it is also the Achilles heel of class reductionism.

I think we must seek the solution elsewhere, firmly rejecting any reductionist assumptions. If we consider the social ensembles that have in capitalist society generally been included in the category 'middle classes', 'intermediary strata', etc. we notice that despite the variety of their insertion in the sphere of economic relations, they do present a basic feature in common: their separation from the dominant relations of production in that society. This means that their contradictions with the dominant bloc are posed, not at the level of the dominant relations of production, but at the level of political and ideological relations which make up the system of domination in that social formation. But as we have seen, *this is not a class contradiction*. This means that, in these sectors, the identity as *the people* plays a much more important role than the identity as *class*. It is obvious that the old and new petty-bourgeoisie are two different classes – or class fraction in the case of the second. Their ideological unity does not therefore reflect a class unity but the fact that popular-democratic interpellations are much more important than their specific class interpellations in the determination of their overall ideological structure. Some differential class interpellations doubtless exist between the distinct sectors of the petty-bourgeoisie, but they are merely secondary. Now since the democratic struggle is always dominated by the class struggle, as we have seen, the popular-democratic ideology of the middle sectors is insufficient to organize its own discourse and can only exist within the ideological discourse of the bourgeoisie or the proletariat. The struggle for the articulation of popular-democratic ideology in class ideological discourses is the basic ideological struggle in capitalist social formations. In this sense, the class imprecision of the formula used by the French Communist Party – 'intermediate wage-earning strata' – although certainly inadequate, is not as mistaken as Poulantzas supposes. It reflects the intuition that a contradiction that is not a class contradiction dominates the political and ideological practice of these sectors – such that if the working class has to condense its class identity and its identity as people in its own ideology, these 'intermediate' sectors have almost exclusively an identity as 'the people'. This means that the middle classes are the natural arena for democratic struggle, and at the same time, as we have seen, the arena *par excellence* of political class struggle. For this is the point at which the identification between 'the people' and classes comes into play, an identification which, far from being given in advance, is the result of a struggle: we would go as far as to say that it is the basic struggle on which depends the resolution of any political crisis under capitalism. We now have, then, all the necessary elements to study the political crisis from which fascism emerged.

The Rise of Fascism: the Crisis of the Power Bloc

Fascism arose from a dual crisis: (1) a crisis of the power bloc which was unable to absorb and neutralize its contradictions with the popular sectors through traditional channels; (2) a crisis of the working class, which was unable to hegemonize popular struggles and fuse popular-democratic ideology and its revolutionary class objectives into a coherent political and ideological practice.

Let us start with the first aspect. The method of neutralizing the power bloc/'people' contradiction typically employed by the bourgeoisie during its ascent, can be synthesized in the term applied to this process in Italian political tradition at the time of Giolitti: *transformism*. By this may be understood the political neutralization of possible opposition from new social groups by co-option of their representative political organizations into the power bloc. From the progressive 'democratization' of the British parliamentary regime to the 'socialist monarchy' of Giolitti, including the Prussian 'conservative revolution', 19th century European history provides us with numerous examples of this mechanism. Its basic ideological function was to absorb the 'people'/power bloc contradictions within the system, preventing popular-democratic interpellations from becoming disarticulated from the dominant ideological discourse. In its most primitive and elemental form, this mechanism functions through *clientelism*: popular-democratic elements are present but only at the level of individualized popular demands. The 'underdog' receives individual satisfaction of his demands from local notables and political bosses, who present themselves as 'friends of the People'. At a higher level this function is fulfilled by popular parties, which become progressively co-opted into the system. In urban sectors especially, where social differentiation increases with industrialization and patriarchal structures enter into crisis, it is necessary to co-opt new groups into the power bloc through more complex mechanisms, to prevent the radicalization of their ideology from putting the existing system of domination in danger. This was essentially, in the prefascist European tradition, the political function of the Radical parties. Finally, the rupture, the moment when the 'people'/power bloc contradiction fails to be neutralized, produces *jacobinism*: 'the people' now emerges not with isolated demands, nor as an organized alternative *within the system*, but as a political alternative to the system itself. Popular-democratic interpellations, from being an ideological element within the political discourse of the bourgeoisie, comes to acquire the maximum possible autonomy compatible with class society. This autonomy is certainly momentary, and sooner or later it dissolves into the reabsorption of the popular interpellations by class ideological discourses; but in any case, this is the moment when the popular-democratic interpellation presents itself, let us say, in virtually pure form.

In this sense, Poulantzas's assertion that jacobinism is a petty-bourgeois ideology can only be accepted if we introduce two series of specifications. Firstly, if jacobinism can be the ideology of the petty-bourgeoisie in exceptional periods of crisis, it is not the normal form of petty-bourgeois ideology. The latter is provided by those ideologies in which popular-democratic interpellations are present, but integrated into the political discourse of the bourgeoisie: in the period we are analyzing, popular clientelism and radical parliamentarism. Secondly, we have to be clear what is petty-bourgeois about jacobinism. It would be mistaken to say that popular-democratic interpellations as such are petty-bourgeois because, as we pointed out before, popular-democratic interpellations are not class ideologies. *What is petty-bourgeois – and here lies the essence of jacobinism – is the conviction that the struggle against the dominant bloc can be carried out as an exclusively democratic struggle, apart from classes.*[40] But the popular-

[40] In characterizing Jacobinism in these terms we are certainly not passing judgement on its progressiveness, which can vary according to differing historical circumstances. Jacobinism was a progressive force in the French Revolution and was, on the contrary, at the service of a deeply reactionary policy under fascism. The justification for using the same term for both kinds of

democratic interpellations must also form an essential part of the ideological and political discourse of the working class. From the socialist point of view, the periods of greatest revolutionary confrontation are not those when class ideology presents itself in its maximum purity but when socialist ideology has fused completely with popular and democratic ideology, when proletarian ideology has succeeded in absorbing all national traditions and in presenting the anti-capitalist struggle as the culmination of democratic struggles and socialism as the common denominator in a total offensive against the dominant bloc. This could not be realized if popular-democratic interpellations had a necessary class belonging. We would say, finally, that even in periods of stability, when the dominant bloc has managed to neutralize its contradictions with 'the people', there always remains a marginal sector, generally in small groups, who try and maintain the integrity of the jacobin programme. Hence popular-democratic interpellations, although predominantly integrated into bourgeois discourse, never appear totally welded to it and always remain in the depth of popular consciousness as a potential source of radicalization. This underground current of political radicalism which runs in parallel and in conflict with 'official' ideology is that represented, in the Italian case, by the Mazzinian and Garibaldian tradition, and any group which sought to present its confrontation with the dominant bloc as radical had necessarily to appeal to this tradition.

If 'transformism' functioned adequately during the long period of economic expansion preceding the First World War, it entered into crisis in Germany and Italy when the war came to an end. An accumulation of contradictions, very adequately described by Poulantzas in what is undoubtedly one of the best parts of the book, conduced to this result. Some of these contradictions were due to relatively external circumstances –

---

situation cannot, therefore, be based on the political contents of the two movements but in the fact that they based their ideology on the radicalization of popular interpellations divorced from the discourses of the dominant classes in the respective social formations. To insist upon this common element is not, I think, to stress a purely formal similarity but to indicate an area of displacements and ideological ambiguities whose clarification is essential for an adequate understanding of fascism.

economic crisis, mobilization for the war of vast masses of men who could not afterwards be reabsorbed by traditional political structures, etc. – but others were the consequence of a hegemonic crisis in the power bloc. This hegemonic crisis was the result of the particular forms which the transition to monopoly capitalism took in Germany and Italy. As Poulantzas points out, this transition was effected, in the German case, in a country where the Bismarckian revolution 'from above' had led to a failure to complete the economic unification of Germany, and where the power of a landowning sector within the State apparatus bore no relation to its real economic weight. In the Italian case, this accumulation of contradictions was even more accentuated because of the political accord represented by the power bloc which had arisen from the Risorgimento: the alliance between the ascendant bourgeoisie of the north and the feudal landowners of the south.

The consequence of this process that is important for our analysis is that monopoly capitalism, to the extent that it occupied an increasingly important place in the economic sphere, found it impossible to assert its political hegemony within the power bloc – an indispensible condition for the political and economic restructuring which capital accumulation required. The existing political system, immobilized by its contradictions, offered no adequate lever by which that transformation could be operated from within. This meant that monopoly capital tried to impose its hegemony through a formula which involved a radical alteration in the form of State. It is important to emphasize, in this respect, that this alteration could not be carried out, either in Germany or Italy, by a military dictatorship. In Germany the Wehrmacht was a bunker dominated by the feudal influence of the Junkers and in Italy the Army was a firm support of the monarchy. The Army, therefore, far from being a possible base of support for the policy of monopoly capital, was one of the forces which it had to neutralize.

If monopoly capital found itself obliged, consequently, radically to confront the existing political system and was therefore unable to base itself firmly on any apparatus within the power bloc itself, it could only achieve its aims by basing itself on a mass movement. But not any mass movement was adaptable to monopoly capital's needs. For this type of adaptation to be effective, two kinds of conditions had to be met. (1) the movement had to be radical, that is to say, presentable as an alternative to the system and not as a bartering formula within the system itself – for otherwise it would have been absorbed within the ruling system and the structural changes required by monopoly capital would have been impossible to carry out; (2) the mobilization had to proceed through interpellations which would prevent any identification between radical popular objectives and socialist objectives, since the latter kind of identification respresented a threat to the capitalist classes as a whole – including monopoly capital.

The post-war crisis provided the first condition in both Germany and Italy. The disarticulation of the traditional mechanisms of control and political neutralization, and the paralysis of a dominant bloc which was beginning to experience its hegemonic crisis with full intensity, led to the collapse of transformism and to the jacobinization of the petty-bourgeoisie. We now know what this involved: the disarticulation of democratic interpellations and the radicalization of those interpellations outside any class discourse. If the crisis provided, then, the first condition necessary for a mass mobilization which would adapt to the needs of monopoly capital, the achievement of the second condition – the production of interpellations which hindered the identification between 'the people' and the working class – was the specific achievement of fascism.

How was the association between fascism and monopoly capital produced? The fascist movement was not by any means an invention of monopoly capital. Poulantzas is perfectly right to minimize the importance of aspects like the financing of fascist gangs. On the one hand, this financing does not prove that fascism was the political formula favoured by big capital; on the other hand, the very fact of financing has been considerably exaggerated and distorted.[41] Monopoly capital maintained alternative policies up to the last minute: in Germany the union effected by the mediation of Schacht took

[41] Cf. Renzo de Felice, *Intervista sul fascismo,* a cura di Michael A. Leeden, Rome, 1975, pp. 48–9.

place late on, when Nazism had come to constitute a power alternative by its own means; and in Italy the industrial sectors thought, up to the very eve of the march on Rome, of a political solution via Orlando, Giolitti or, particularly, Salandra, in which the fascists would occupy only a subordinate position. Furthermore, in every circumstance where monopoly capital was not forced to accept the fascist solution, it preferred not to do so; in some cases it could impose its hegemony through solutions within the parliamentary system itself (England, France, etc.); in other cases it realized it through military dictatorships (as in many Latin-American countries at present). In those countries where fascism did not become a mass movement, its relations with monopoly capital have been non-existent: it would be absurd to suggest that Sir Oswald Mosley or Jose Antonio Primo de Rivera were expressions of monopoly capital.

But, in any case, fascism provided the necessary condition for monopoly capital to make use of a mass mobilization against the traditional system of power: the guarantee that popular-democratic interpellations would remain disconnected from any socialist perspective. This aim was realized by fascism through a dual ideological transformation: (1) at the level of the 'people'/power bloc contradiction there occurred the unification of the ensemble of popular interpellations through a subject which eliminated the very possibility of the class struggle. For example: the radicalized German petty-bourgeoisie which was experiencing in a confused way the post-war crisis, the iniquity of the Versailles Treaty, inflation, foreign occupation, etc., was interpellated by nazism as a *race*. All the anti-plutocratic, nationalist, democratic aspects, that is to say all those elements which constituted the identity of the dominated classes as '*people*', and which thus expressed their contradiction with the power bloc, were present in Nazi discourse, but the interpellated subject was a racial one. Through this identification of popular traditions with racism, a dual aim was achieved: all the jacobin radicalism proper to a radical confrontation with the system was retained, whilst its channeling in a socialist direction is obstructed. (2) Class interpellations were retained but their meaning at the political level was denied: that is the class struggle was denied. The expression of this ideological transformation was corporativism. The essential contradiction at the level of political struggle is, as we have seen, the 'people'/power bloc contradiction; thus the political struggle of the working class must tend to realize a total identity between popular struggle and socialist struggle, and the political struggle of the bourgeoisie tends to maintain the separation between the two, so that the working class may be politically neutralized. This political neutralization operates through *reformism* and *trade-unionism* in a liberal parliamentary régime: this allows the working class to present itself as a political alternative to the country as a whole insofar as its aims are reforms internal to the system itself. In corporativism, on the contrary, '*people*' and *class* come to be strictly separated and no common zone between them is tolerated. (Of course, in Nazi discourse a German worker was interpellated as German and as a worker; but what was not tolerated was any assertion that the workers were the authentic representatives of the historic interests of the German people).

Now if class interpellations were maintained/neutralized in the form of corporativism, the jacobin and anti-status quo character of fascist ideology was retained. The reason for this seems clear: as we pointed out before, without jacobinism the old system of power would have tended to reconstruct itself and the reorganization of the State required by the monopoly fraction could not be effected.[42] Naturally the maintenance of jacobin interpellations was a dangerous game, since they could easily slip towards an effective anti-capitalism. In the phase prior to the seizure of power the class struggle had penetrated

[42] Hence the revolutionary and anti-status quo rhetoric which persisted in fascism up to the last moment and which was sometimes reflected in a feeling of sharing formal revolutionary values with communist leaders. In September 1943, Goebbels wrote in his diary: '"Il Duce" has not drawn the moral conclusions from the Italian catastrophe that the Führer was expecting. . . . He is not a revolutionary of the temper of the Führer or Stalin. He is so bound to his people, so completely Italian, that he lacks the necessary qualities for a revolutionary of world stature'. In April 1945, when Mussolini was abandoning the prefecture of Milan and closing the cycle of Italian fascism, Bombacci noted: 'What else would I need? . . . I am expert in these matters. I was in Lenin's office in Petersburg when the white troops of Yudenitch were advancing on the city and we were preparing to leave, as we were doing today' (cited in F. W. Deakin, *The Brutal Friendship,* London, 1968, p. 811).

the fascist movements themselves and it was only through a harsh process of internal purges that the danger of an anti-capitalist orientation could be averted. Suffice it to note that as late as the autumn of 1930 the Nazi representatives Strasser, Feder and Frick presented a proposed law demanding a 4% ceiling on all interest rates, the expropriation of the holdings of 'banking and finance magnates' with no compensation, and the nationalization of the big banks. Hitler obliged his deputies to withdraw the project. The same project, word for word, was then presented by the Communist deputies and the Nazi representatives were forced by Hitler to vote against. To avoid the possibility of this type of development away from 'official jacobinism' necessitated, after the seizure of power, bloody purges, constant ideological vigilance and generalized repression. In Italy, the neutralization of possible anti-capitalist tendencies in the fascist left was relatively easier than in Germany, because the 'extreme' line of Italian fascism was sustained by the Mazzinian and Garibaldian tradition, that is to say, by an autochthonous bourgeois radical tradition. In Germany, by contrast, the absence of this tradition compelled the Nazi left to take its constitutive elements largely from the socialist tradition, for which worker interpellations had a much greater importance. A comparative analysis of the speeches of Strasser and Farinacci leaves little doubt in this respect.

Can it be said that with the coming to power of fascism and with the elimination of its radical sectors there took place a complete fusion between the fascist movement and monopoly capital, that – to make the usual distinction – any differentiation between the *movement* and the *régime* was obliterated? As we know, the response of the Comintern was emphatically in the affirmative, and that of Poulantzas, despite its formal opposition to the Comintern conception, seems to me to move rather in the same direction. In this way an extremely complex phenomenon, which operated differently in Italy and Germany, is greatly over-simplified. In Germany, without doubt, the maximum fusion was produced. But it is necessary to introduce some distinctions at this point. The consequent application of an economic policy based on the long-term interests of monopoly capital – such as Nazism undoubtedly implemented – did not mean that monopoly capital directly controlled political power. The price which monopoly capital had to pay to impose the economic transformation needed for its expansion was precisely the existence of a kind of capitalist State whose relative autonomy from the dominant economic sectors was much greater than would have been the case with a parliamentary regime. As Poulantzas correctly notes, the political importance of the fusion between big capital and certain high echelons of the Nazi hierarchy (such as Goering) has often been exaggerated. It is obvious that monopoly capital was trying through these co-options to create a strong pressure group within the Nazi State; but to deduce from these the total subordination of the Nazi State to the dictates of big capital is something quite different, and goes against a good deal of the historical evidence. I think that Poulantzas ultimately falls into the same mistake as the Comintern, in rejecting without any justification observations and analyses which tend to show, precisely, the relative autonomy of the Nazi State: without the latter, the war economy could not have been organized in the way it was, and it is certainly difficult to imagine that big capital was promoting the suicidal politics of Hitler in the final stage of the war.

In Italy the fusion between movement and regime was less and the fascist 'left' was not totally eliminated. The absorption of the 'ancien regime' by the fascist State was not complete and the monarchy always maintained itself as a political alternative in case a crisis should threaten the very bases of the State. It is characteristic, in this sense, that Farinacci and the radical sectors of fascism presented themselves as anti-monarchical, and as direct opponents of the fusion between the fascist State and the interests of big capital – a collusion that led to the frustration of the jacobin aspirations which had formed the initial impulse of the movement.[43] The fascist right, by contrast, which presented itself as the direct ally of monopoly capital, tended to maintain to the fullest possible extent the traditional institutions and to progressively institutional-

[43] Cf. in this regard the various volumes of Renzo de Felice's monumental biography of Mussolini, especially the early ones: *Mussolini il rivoluzionario (1883–1920)*, Turin, 1965; *Mussolini il fascista: la Concuista del potere (1921–1925)*, Turin, 1966; *Mussolini il fascista: l'organizzazione dello Stato fascista.*

ize and liberalize the regime. The regime constantly oscillated between these two alternatives, between these two 'souls', according to De Felice's expression, without being able totally to absorb and condense either of them, in the way that Hitler had done. During the Matteotti crisis it was the massive mobilization of radical fascism which saved the regime; during the years of consolidation, on the contrary, institutionalist tendencies prevailed and, with the crisis of the fascist State in 1943, both currents experienced a final division: institutionalist fascism, led by Dino Grandi, provoked the fall of Mussolini and emigrated with the King to the South supported by every sector of Italian capitalism; radical fascism attempted on the contrary, the adventure of the Salò Republic: a petty-bourgeois utopia based on the adoption without concessions of the radical jacobin traditions of Mazzini and Garibaldi, with all its links with autochthonous capitalism broken, and based on the massive fact of German occupation.

We have shown, then, how the hegemonic crisis of the power bloc led in both Italy and Germany to a fascist solution. A basic point remains to be clarified, however: why was fascism successful in separating 'people' and working class? Why was the jacobinism of the petty-bourgeoisie not absorbed by working class political discourse into a radical confrontation with the power bloc? This leads us to the second aspect of the crisis from which fascism emerged: the crisis of the working class. *Our thesis is that if fascism was possible it was because the working class, both in its reformist and its revolutionary sectors, had abandoned the arena of popular-democratic struggle.*

The Rise of Fascism: the Crisis of the Working Class

In his book, Poulantzas analyzes the crisis of the workers' movement which contributed to the emergence of fascism. In studying the errors and deviations which led to the crisis, he summarizes them into one basic error that was at the root of them all: economism. Poulantzas' critique of economism is penetrating and convincing, and it would be difficult to disagree with most of his assertions. However, there is a basic deficiency in his analysis: Poulantzas remains tied to the basic assumptions of his theoretical approach and, consequently, has criticized the economism of the Comintern whilst retaining its class reductionism. That it is possible to maintain class reductionism whilst criticizing economic determinism is something to which the history of 20th century Marxism bears ample witness: we only have to think of Lukács, Korsch and in general all those tendencies which stress the importance and specificity of superstructures or consciousness, but who assign to them a strict class belonging. In Poulantzas's case, the consequence is as we have pointed out earlier: that he has ignored the specific autonomy of popular-democratic interpellations, without which the fascist phenomenon is unintelligible. Hence his critique of economism is unilateral and inadequate, and cannot go beyond purely and simply asserting the errors of the conceptions he is criticizing. Even if we would agree with Poulantzas that economism is the source of all the errors of the workers' movement in the fascist period, a basic question remains unanswered: why were the workers' movement and the Comintern economist? Poulantzas provides no answer apart from sporadic references to 'residues' from the political practice of the Second International,[44] allusions to subjective errors, and a reference to the class struggle in the USSR which explains nothing since – as Poulantzas asserts himself – its influence on the European Communist movement was transmitted through the specific economism of the latter. The conclusion is obvious: if economism is the manifestation of a crisis of the working class, it is not possible to explain this crisis via a mere critique of economism; it is necessary to deepen the analysis and situate the root and origin of this crisis in the domain of class practices.

We can begin by answering our question: why was the jacobinism of the petty-bourgeoisie not articulated with socialist political discourse? The answer is that socialist political discourse had been structured in such a way that it excluded as a matter of principle its articulation with any interpellation which was not a class interpellation. To understand why this was so we have to remember that in its origins, the workers'

[44] The limitations of Poulantzas's conception in this aspect have been correctly pointed out by Anthony Cutler, 'Fascism and Political Theory', *Theoretical Practice*, no 2, April, 1971, pp. 5–15.

movement developed and matured in Europe on the basis of an absolutely intransigent maintenance of the class barrier. The workers' movement was at such an early stage of development and so subjected to the influences of the bourgeoisie, that the only way of assuring its class identity was to transform the class barrier into an absolute criterion of separation between the working class and the rest of society. It was especially necessary to break working class interpellations from diffuse popular interpellations since the working class had frequently been mobilized and frustrated by the populism of bourgeois politicians. Diffuse popular ideologies had to be 'exposed' so that they did not hinder the construction of a class ideology. The specific mechanism of this exposure was to present any diffuse popular content as an element of the ideology of one of the rival classes: the bourgeoisie, the petty-bourgeoisie, the feudal landowners, etc. In this way the revolutionary determination and, at the same time, the historical immaturity of the working class generated political and ideological practices which expressed themselves in class reductionism. Thus the class criterion came to be decisive at all levels: political life, family relations, aesthetics, etc.; intra-party and intra-union relations had to be a microcosm which prefigured future society. In this perspective, any possible autonomy of popular-democratic struggles was excluded *ab initio*: the democratic struggle might, at most, be an index of an unrealized bourgeois task and thus the occasion for a *class front* with the bourgeoisie for limited objectives.

In this initial phase, one task took priority over all the others: the organization of the unions and the economic struggle of the working class. The working class began, then, to organize itself as a pressure group within bourgeois society. Class reductionism functioned around the relations of production and the *de facto* priority of the economic struggle. How were these pressure group activities linked to the aspirations of the working class to organize a socialist society in the future? This is the point at which economism entered the picture: (1) it was thought that the dynamic of capitalist accumulation led to the proletarianization of the middle sectors and of the peasantry[45] so that, in defending its own class interests, the

[45] As we know, this conclusion is not a necessary deduction from Marx's analysis. But what is important for our subject is that numerous sectors of the

working class would end by defending the interests of society as a whole; (2) the purely economic contradictions inherent in capitalist accumulation would provoke, by the simple unfolding of its internal mechanism, the crisis of the system. In this way the microcosms represented by the economic struggle held the key to all the secrets of future development. Logical deduction from the premises of Volume 1 of *Capital* led to the promise of a socialist society. Austro-Marxism, Rosa Luxemburg's demonstration of the impossibility of capital accumulation in a closed system and her consequent theory of collapse, the manipulation of the schemas of expanded reproduction by Henryk Grossman, predicting the exact year when capitalism would perish, are all testimonies to an intellectual style in which economism came to be a basic mechanism of class reductionism.

To criticize economism, then, outside the overall ideological context to which it belongs – class reductionism – is like trying to understand the meaning of a piece of machinery in isolation from the engine of which it is a part. Hence, Poulantzas cannot explain why economism was a basic ideological component of the workers' movement in the period of the emergence of fascism, and he tries to overcome this difficulty by the purely additive introduction of political and ideological criteria in the determination of classes. (With which he does not solve the problems he tackles but multiplies them on ever broader levels.)

Class reductionism, then, was closely linked to the class practices of the workers' movement before the First World War. In the immediate post-war period it had still not been overcome: the workers' movement remained dominated by a narrow class perspective, and it lacked any hegemonic will in relation to the exploited classes as a whole. For the reformist fraction the question was one of reconstructing the machinery of the bourgeois State as soon as possible, to re-establish the conditions of negotiation which had enabled the working class to obtain increasing benefits. For the revolutionary fraction the aim was to carry out a proletarian revolution and install a soviet regime. But in both cases, exclusively class policies were

---

workers' movement experienced this prognosis as a necessary consequence of Marxist analysis.

pursued, which totally ignored the problem of popular-democratic struggles. Hence the radicalization of the middle classes and the crisis of transformism confronted the working class parties with a completely new situation for which they had, in fact, no answer. Consequently, they did not even try to link the radical jacobinism of the middle classes to socialist discourse: they maintained themselves in a pure class perspective which led to their political suicide. Fascism, in this sense, was the result of a crisis of the working class – a crisis not rooted in the working class's incapability of carrying out a proletarian revolution in Italy or Germany, but in its incapability of presenting itself to the dominated classes as a whole as a hegemonic popular alternative, in the course of the most serious crisis that the system of capitalist domination had experienced until then in Europe. As a result, the popular interpellations of the middle classes were absorbed and neutralized in the way we have described by fascist political discourse, which put them at the service of the new monopoly fraction. But the process also had repercussions at the level of the working class. As we have said, the working class has a dual identity: as class and as 'the people'. The failure of the various class attempts – revolutionary or reformist – to overcome the crisis led to the demoralization and demobilization of the working class; the lack of articulation of popular interpellations with socialist discourse left this flank increasingly exposed to the ideological influence of fascism. From this develops a fact to which Poulantzas alludes: the implantation of fascism in part of the working class and the political neutralization of the working class as a whole.

If there was a clear 'manifest destiny' for any European working class at the end of the First World War, it was that of the German working class. The crisis of the dominant ideology was revealed, as every crisis is, in the disarticulation of its constituent interpellations. On the one hand the authority and prestige of the dominant power bloc appeared to be seriously damaged; on the other hand, nationalist agitation amongst the middle classes took an increasingly plebeian and anti-capitalist trait. This is the fissure through which Hitlerism penetrated, and this penetration was a consequence of the failure of the working class to keep its rendezvous with History. The working class should have presented itself as the force which would lead the historic struggles of the German people to their conclusion, and to socialism as their consummation; it should have pointed to the limitations of Prussianism, whose ambiguities and compromises with the old dominant classes had led to the national catastrophe, and it should have made an appeal to all popular sectors to fight for a national renaissance which could be condensed in common ideological symbols: Nationalism, Socialism and Democracy.[46] (The crisis had provoked the disarticulation of the nationalist and the authoritarian interpellations characteristic of the old Prussianism, i.e., the latter had lost its historic rights to be considered outright as representing the national interests; on the other hand, the fact that a plebeian agitator such as Hitler – whom Hindenburg disdainfully referred to as the Austrian corporal – named his movement 'National-Socialism', is an eloquent proof that these two words, in the mind of the masses, tended to be condensed spontaneously). A hegemonic will on the part of the working class would have had a great impact on the jacobinized petty-bourgeoisie and would have enabled their protest to be oriented in a socialist direction. Even had Hitler emerged, he would not have had the monopoly of popular and nationalist language which he enjoyed; the left-wing sectors of his movement, disappointed by his capitulations to the capitalist classes, would have found an alternative pole of regroupment, and monopoly capital would in the end have been much less prepared to put its bets on an ideological alternative whose system of interpellations constituted an area of debate with the communist movement. But nothing of the sort happened, and the abandonment of the arena of popular-democratic struggle by the working class left the way open for fascism. It therefore seems incredible that Poulantzas criticizes what was one of the few moments in which the German Communist movement sensed the necessity to carry out national and democratic

[46] The fact that the German popular interpellations, owing to the specific historic development of the country, have had a strong nationalist component, does not mean to say that in every case popular interpellations are necessarily nationalistic. In the British case, for example, the nationalist element is far less present – indeed the universalist element is predominant in democratic ideology. Besides, one must not confuse nationalism and national traditions.

agitation: the Schlageter line. It is true that in this formulation there were many opportunist elements and that its sporadic application only helped to weaken the German working class faced with Nazism. But, in the first place, the opportunist elements resulted from the fact that this line was conceived as a *concession* to the petty-bourgeoisie because of the class reductionism which dominated Comintern policies, and secondly, it is obvious that the democratic struggle could only produce negative effects if it was carried out in a sporadic zig-zagging manner and not as a wide-ranging endeavour to articulate popular-democratic and socialist interpellations. The correct position would have been to deepen this line and carry it to its logical conclusion: the abandonment of class reductionism. If this direction was not followed, it was not because of any subjective errors but because of the structural situation of immaturity which we have described, which determined the overall class practices of the workers' movement.

A criticism similar to that of Poulantzas was made, at the time of the rise of Nazism, by Leon Trotsky. He wrote in 1931, referring to the 'Nationalist' line of the German Communist Party: 'It is understood that every great revolution is a people's or a national revolution, in the sense that it unites around the revolutionary class all the virile and creative forces of the nation and reconstructs the nation around a new core. But this is not a slogan; it is a sociological description of the revolution, which requires, moreover, precise and concrete definition. As a slogan, it is inane and charlatanism, market competition with the fascists, paid for at the price of injecting confusion into the mind of the workers . . . The fascist Strasser says 95 per cent of the people are interested in the revolution, consequently it is not a class revolution but a people's revolution. Thälmann sings in chorus. In reality, the worker-Communist should say to the fascist worker: of course, 95 per cent of the population, if not 98 per cent is exploited by finance capital. But this exploitation is organized hierarchially: there are exploiters, there are sub-exploiters, sub-sub-exploiters, etc. Only thanks to this hierarchy do the super-exploiters keep in subjection the majority of the nation. In order that the nation should indeed be able to reconstruct itself around a new class core, it must be reconstructed ideologically and this can be achieved only if the proletariat does not dissolve itself into the "people", into the "nation", but on the contrary develops a programme of *its* proletarian revolution and compels the petty-bourgeoisie to choose between the two regimes'.[47] It would be difficult to find a more complete formulation of class reductionism: (1) the specificity of the contradiction people/power bloc is negated and only class contradictions are accepted (exploiters, sub-exploiters, sub-sub-exploiters, etc.); (2) the specificity and autonomy of the popular-democratic ideologies obviously disappears, and the latter are reduced to mere slogans or charlatanism; (3) there are only two extreme possibilities: either a class ideology in all its purity or the dissolution of the proletariat in 'the people' – thereby, the possibility of a class articulation of popular ideologies is denied; (4) consequently, we can be hardly surprised by the political conclusion of this reductionist sectarianism: the *proletarian* revolution is the only aim that the working class can pose to the middle classes.

Thälmann's policy was doubtless mistaken, in so far as it reduced a *fundamental long-term strategic line,* such as the fusion between socialism and popular-democratic ideology, to a *mere circumstantial tactic* to win the electoral support of the petty bourgeoisie. But this was not Trotsky's critique. Trotsky simply denied the need for such a fusion and confined himself to a pure class ideology. It has been commonly asserted that Trotsky was one of the few revolutionary Marxists who understood the danger of Nazism and posed a correct strategy for the working class. But in this I think there is a fundamental misunderstanding: it is true that Trotsky perceived more acutely than the Comintern the nature of Nazism, its roots in the petty-bourgeoisie and the deadly peril it involved for the workers' movement; it is also true that his calls for the unity of action with social-democracy showed a remarkable clairvoyance compared with the political blindness of the 'social-fascism' line. But his accuracy was limited to the formulation of a correct defensive line when in all essentials Fascism had already won the battle for the political conquest of the petty-bourgeoisie. The idea that in Germany any advance towards

[47] 'Against National Communism: Lessons of the Red Referendum', in *The Struggle against fascism in Germany*, London, 1975, p. 62. Cf. also 'Problems of the Italian Revolution', in *Writings of Leon Trotsky (1930),* New York, 1975.

socialism was dependent on the alliance between the working class and the middle class, and that such an alliance required the ideological fusion of Nationalism, Socialism and Democracy, is not only alien but antagonistic to the bases of Trotsky's thinking. His misunderstanding of the nature of the popular-democratic struggle leaves little doubt that a Trotskyist leadership of the German Communist Party would have made the same strategic errors as the Comintern and that it would have been, consequently, equally impotent to stop the advance of Nazism.

In Italy the situation was even clearer. It was necessary to present the working class as the hegemonic class for all the popular forces radicalized by the crisis of transformism. The working class had to present itself as the historical realizer of incompleted tasks of the Risorgimento. But for the communist leadership of Bordiga, the strictest 'classism' had to dominate the political practice of the party – Mazzinian and Garibaldian jacobinism could only be ideologies of rival classes. Radical jacobinism was expressed in Italy by a magic formula in the immediate post-war period: the demand for a Constituent Assembly which would establish the foundations of a reorganization of the Italian State. This old formula of the Risorgimento had become transformed into the essential demand of all forces opposed to the dominant power bloc. Yet the maximalist sector of the Socialist Party and the Communist Party opposed the Constituent Assembly and counterposed the setting-up of soviets. Naturally this class isolationism led to the defeat of the workers' movement and the absorption of radical jacobin interpellations by fascism.[48] Gramsci always consider-

[48] Giorgio Amendola has said recently: 'I would like to call attention to another element which during the war (the First World War, E. L.) constituted a premise for the development of the political struggle in the post-war period, i.e. the formation around Salandra of the Fascio Nazionale in December 1917. This undifferentiated 'fascio' of forces which spread from the Conservatives, such as Salandra, to the Nationalists, to the Anarcho-syndicalists, to Mussolini, including the Democratic Interventionists, and which had a monopoly of patriotism, was directed by the forces of the right. For the neutralist forces did not at that time know how to bring forward the patriotic and the nationalist reasons for their neutralism ... This fact, on the one hand, damaged the neutralist forces during the post-war period, preventing them from playing the nationalist card, and on the other hand it presented the patriotic banner to this "fascio" of heterogeneous forces. Mussolini, at one point, named his journal

ed that the rejection of the Constituent Assembly formula had been a major error of the Communist Party in the pre-fascist period. Already in 1924 he was writing: 'Is it likely that the slogan of the Constituent Assembly will become current again? If it is, what should be our position on this? Briefly, the present situation must have a political solution. What is the most probable form that such a solution will take? Is it possible to think that we shall pass from fascism to the dictatorship of the proletariat? What intermediate phases are likely or probable? I think that in the crisis the country is going through, the party which has the advantage will be the one which best understands this necessary process of transition'.[49] The formula of the Constituent Assembly was from then on central to Gramsci's political conception. We can see in it, in embryo, the great ideological themes which were to dominate the political practice of the Italian Communist Party after the war of liberation.

Let us remark, to conclude this point, that the parallelism we have used in the presentation of the German and Italian cases, must not lead to the false conclusion that all countries have popular-democratic traditions that are equivalent in

---

the journal of the "fascio" of workers, fighters and producers and took the word "fascio", a word which had a tradition even in the leftist movement, dating from the Sicilian Fasci of 1892–94, and which describes quite appropriately the possible unity of heterogeneous forces in a country of such diversity as Italy. . . .' (*Intervista sull'antifascismo*, Bari, 1976, pp. 30–1).

[49] Cf. Palmiro Togliatti, *La formazzione del gruppo dirigente del Partito Communista Italiano,* Rome, 1962, p. 246. Certain commentators have endeavoured to interpret the whole of the experience of the 'bienio rosso' (1919–20) as a frustrated democratic revolution. Pietro Nenni, for example, underlines in connection with this subject the importance of the agitation for the Constituent Assembly, while Angelo Tasca (*Nascita e avvento del fascismo,* Bari, 1965) and Leo Valiani 'La storia del fascismo nella problematica della storia contemporacea e nella biografia di Mussolini', *Rivista Storica Italiana,* Giugno, 1967, pp. 459–81) refer to the possibility of a convergence with D'Annunzio's 'patriotic subversivism'. Giovanni Sabbatucci, who has recently commented on both theses – and has, in our mind, cast them aside much too quickly – nonetheless concludes also by affirming the possibilities of a successful democratic alliance: 'There were no structural impediments caused by any irremediable contrast of interests, to the possibility of a democratic alliance between the workers, peasants and vast numbers of the middle sectors. There were, as has been stated, deep splits, serious obstacles, but always of a contingent nature: to remove these obstacles was the task – difficult, but unavoidable – of the progressive political forces, and in particular, of the workers' movement'. (*La crisi italiana del primo dopoguerra,* Bari, 1976, p. 24.)

their degree of dissociation from the dominant bourgeois discourse and in their potential for incorporation in the socialist discourse. Barrington Moore has shown, for instance,[50] the way in which the historic development of the Prussian State favoured an increasing symbiosis between authoritarianism and nationalism and consequently hindered the bourgeois revolution from adopting a democratic model. Moreover, the differences between Italy and Germany in this respect, are quite notable. As is clear from our preceding analysis, the popular-democratic tradition in Italy was much stronger than in Germany and it was less absorbed into the ideological discourse of the dominant classes. Thereby the alternative articulation of popular interpellations with the ideological discourse of the working class, was comparatively easier in Italy than in Germany. This does not mean to say, nevertheless, that this was an *impossible* task in Germany – the post-war crisis proves, as we have seen, that this was not the case – but only that the German working class had to confront such a task with a more ill-equipped ideological arsenal than the Italian proletariat. In this sense, Barrington Moore's explanation appears biased – notwithstanding its undeniable interest – by the abuse of a type of analysis which seems to imply that from the 15th century till Hitler, authoritarianism in Germany constituted a fate which did not permit alternative lines of development. In this way the coherence and degree of condensation of the ideologies of the dominant bloc are overestimated while the role of the popular-democratic ideologies is extremely underestimated. But the latter, even if in a marginal and certainly not hegemonic way, always exist and emerge at the time of a crisis. As Lenin said: 'The *elements* of democratic and socialist culture are present, if only in a rudimentary form, in every national culture . . . But *every* nation possesses a bourgeois culture, in the form, not merely of " elements" but of the dominant culture'.[51]

[50] Barrington Moore Jr., *Social Origins of Dictatorship and Democracy*.
[51] V. I. Lenin, 'Critical Notes on the National Question', *Collected Works*, vol. 20, p. 24.

The Political Lessons of Fascism

If the foregoing analysis is correct, fascism arose from a dual crisis: a crisis of the dominant sectors who were incapable of neutralizing by traditional methods the jacobin potential of popular-democratic interpellations; a crisis of the working class which was incapable of articulating them in socialist political discourse. It may seem that with this analysis we are giving excessive weight to the incidence of ideology in the emergence of fascism. But I do not think this is the case. The crisis of the dominant classes only becomes intelligible if it is referred to the contradictions of the process of capitalist accumulation, to the influence of the imperialist war on this process, to the economic crisis, etc. We do not intend to cast doubt on the priority of production relations in the ultimate determination of historical processes. What we wish to say is that the process of social reproduction is not just the reproduction of the dominant mode of production but also of its conditions, one of which is ideology; and that the greater the importance in a social formation of those sectors which do not participate directly in dominant production relations, the greater will be the importance and relative autonomy of ideological processes for social reproduction as a whole. The growing social and political weight of the 'middle classes', that is to say, of sectors in whose general ideological structure popular interpellations play a much more important role than those of class, determined at the same time a broader extension of the arena of democratic struggle, and the growing importance of ideological struggle within the general arena of class struggle. For the Marxism of the Second International the importance of these sectors would constantly diminish, from which was derived, as we have seen, a policy in which class reductionism and economism played a decisive role. But the prediction was shown to be false: under the conditions of monopoly capitalism, the importance of these sectors has tended constantly to increase. The triumph of fascism was the first evidence of this unexpected situation, and in the crisis which determined its coming to power, ideological factors played a fundamental role. Hence the proliferation of psychological and psychoanalytical theories which attempted to explain the origin and nature of fascism: behind them lay the confused intuition that fascism was the result of processes in which ideology was playing a much more autonomous and decisive role than in other contemporary political phenomena. Hence also the analyses which tended to present fascism as the interruption and distortion of a 'normal' historical process – of course, normality consisted in a political conduct strictly determined by sectoral economic interests. Hence – since even in the most mistaken theories a grain of truth is hidden – the fact which the theories of totalitarianism tried to express: in the assertion that in fascism the individual acted as *mass* and not as *class*, lay hidden the intuition that it was not interpellations as *class* but interpellations as '*people*' which dominated fascist political discourse.[52] (Obviously this fact was deformed by the theorists of totalitarianism by the postulation of a mythical 'individual', totally separated from traditional ties.)

Fascism was the crisis of maturity of the workers' movement. Before fascism, the two poles of the reform-revolution alternative defined each other in terms of an essentially intra-class perspective. After it, this perspective began to change. In 1944 a lucid reformist theorist, Adolf Sturmthal, stressed what had, in his view, been the major error of the workers' movement in the inter-war years: its pressure group mentality and its inability to present itself to the popular classes as a whole as a political alternative. He wrote: 'I intend to show that European labour, far from "mixing too much with politics", was not sufficiently politically minded, and hesitated to accept real political responsibility commensurate with the political and social pressure which it exercized'. Referring to the possible objection that the workers' movement participated in elections, spoke of socialism, etc., he comments: 'All this, however, was largely surface activity. Scraping below it, we would find, well hidden in the maze of political action but determining its content, the same pressure group mentality that is characteristic of American labour. For most Socialists, during the en-

[52] We disagree, in this sense, with Poulantzas's claim that fascism had a totally distinct political discourse for each social sector. The essence of the fascist political discourse consisted, on the contrary, in sectoralizing all class interpellations and subordinating it to interpellations conceived in terms of society as a whole (such as in the example of racism that we gave before).

tire period between the two wars, and most Communists after 1923, Socialism was a distant objective which had little influence upon present-day action. Their actual objective was the defence of the interests of industrial workers in much the same way as the American unions represented the interests of their members. They realized that their Socialist programme could be carried out only after labour had achieved full power. Their immediate activity was thus restricted to immediate demands which fell into two types: social demands as advocated by and for the trade-unions, and democratic demands as proclaimed by all democratic elements, labour and bourgeois alike. These were their real objectives until the day should come when, with full powers in their hands, they could create a Socialist society. To all intents and purposes, therefore, the labour parties acted as pressure groups . . . Unfortunately the labour parties, though thinking and acting as pressure groups, were political parties, and as such were called upon to form governments, whether through a revolutionary process, as in Central Europe in 1918, or according to the rules of parliamentarism. When confronted with governmental responsibilities, the narrowness of the range of problems for which labour offered constructive solutions became apparent. This lack applied to practically all labour parties . . . although reference to the Socialist objectives of the movements – in other words rather than deeds – tended to obscure this conspicuous narrowness of scope of the parties' real interests'.[53]

After the war, European Social-Democratic parties tried to overcome this limitation with a characteristic formula: acceptance of the pressure-group character of the workers' movement as permanent, and acquiescence in a total fusion between popular-democratic interpellations and bourgeois liberal ideology. In contrast to the old Social-Democracy, which considered the working class as the hegemonic class in a future socialist society and tried through economism to create a bridge between these remote perspectives and the trade-unionist and reformist activity of the present, and in contrast to fascism which sectoralized class demands and dis-

[53] A. Sturmthal, *The Tragedy of European Labour, 1918–1939*, New York, 1951, p. 37.

articulated popular interpellations from liberal bourgeois ideology, Social-Democracy today is based on a dual ideological movement. It accepts that the working class is a mere pressure group *and will always be so*, that is to say, that the working class has no long-term political objectives of its own, as was the case for Social-Democracy in the fascist period. At the same time, it does not struggle to disarticulate popular-democratic interpellations from liberal bourgeois discourse but, on the contrary, to assert the inseparable unity between them and to present its own political programme as a relatively more 'democratic' and 'redistributive' alternative within that discourse. Contemporary Social-Democracy, then, has overcome the pressure group mentality of the old socialism via its transformation into a bourgeois party like the others. The distance between '*the people*' and *class* is maintained – albeit by other means – as strictly as in fascism and certainly much more than in Social-Democracy between the wars. The transition represented by Hugh Gaitskell in England or Ollenhauer and Willy Brandt in Germany is characteristic in this respect. Once this separation between the people and class was carried out, Social-Democracy was naturally able to maintain the closest links with a particular pressure-group such as the trade-unions.

In the Communist movement, the attempt to overcome class reductionism occurred along different lines. Albeit in an imperfect and zig-zag way, subjected to Stalinist pressure and the turns of Soviet foreign policy, various tendencies in the Communist movement tried to orient towards a fusion between socialism and popular-democratic ideology. The abandonment by the Comintern of the ultra-left sectarianism of the 'social-fascist' period created a political space which enabled some Communist leaderships to reorient their policies in this direction. The Seventh Congress of the Comintern constituted the dividing line in this respect.[54] In a report to it, notable in many

[54] The adoption of this new line on the part of the Comintern in its VII Congress implied, of course, self-criticism with respect of the period of 'Social-Fascism'. Poulantzas rightly says in his book that such self-criticism was totally insufficient, and from it stemmed a long series of errors and deviations. The problem in fact exceeds the theme of this paper, but I would like in any case to make a few points. To propagate the need for a democratic front, while

ways, Dimitrov stated: 'One of the weakest aspects of the anti-fascist struggle of our Parties is that they *react inadequately and too slowly to the demagogy of fascism,* and to this day continue to neglect the problem of the struggle against fascist ideology . . . The fascists are rummaging through the entire history of every nation so as to be able to pose as the heirs and continuators of all that was exalted and heroic in its past, while all that was degrading or offensive to the national sentiments of the people they make use of as weapons against the enemies of fascism. Hundreds of books are being published in Germany with only one aim – to falsify the history of the German people and give it a fascist complexion . . . Mussolini makes every effort to make capital for himself out of the heroic figure of Garibaldi. The French fascists bring to the fore as their heroine Joan of Arc. The American fascists appeal to the traditions of the American War of Independence, the tradition of Washington and Lincoln. The Bulgarian fascists make use of the national liberation movements of the seventies and its heroes beloved by the people, Vasil Lavsky, Stephen Karaj and others.

'Communists who suppose that all this has nothing to do with the cause of the working class, who do nothing to enlighten the masses on the past of their people, in a historically

---

at the same time asserting the bourgeois character of democratic banners, can only lead to a right wing deviation. Stalinist policy contributed to this deviation, since it was more interested in the presence in power of bourgeois governments willing to establish alliances with the Soviet Union, than in promoting proletarian hegemony in the democratic fronts. Therefore, if the historic experience of the working class encountered an ideological barrier in class reductionism, Stalinist policy contributed to reinforcing such barriers. Nevertheless, the political line which emerged from the VII Congress of the Comintern allowed for a different reading: it made it possible to affirm the non-class character of democratic banners and, consequently, the struggle for proletarian hegemony within the democratic fronts. The mere possibility of this interpretation involved a fundamental advance: while the political line of 'social-fascism' only led to mistakes and failures, the line of the VII Congress yielded – together with the deviations we mentioned previously – a vast number of successful experiences, ranging from the triumph of the Yugoslav Revolution to Togliatti's transformation of the Italian Communist party in a mass movement. It is therefore understandable why the Italian Communists go back to the VII Congress of the Comintern when they now wish to trace the origins of their present strategic line. (Cf., Luciano Gruppi, *Togliatti e la via italiana al socialismo,* Roma, 1974, especially Chapter I 'Dal fronte popolare all'unita nazionale antifascista'.)

correct fashion, in a genuinely Marxist, a Leninist-Marxist, a Leninist-Stalinist spirit, who do nothing to *link up the present struggle with the people's revolutionary traditions and past* – voluntarily hand over to the fascist falsifiers all that is valuable in the historical past of the nation, that the fascist may dupe the masses.

'No comrades, *we are concerned with every important question, not only of the present and future, but also of the past of our own people.* We Communists do not pursue a narrow policy based on the craft interest of the workers. We are not narrow-minded trade union functionaries, or leaders of mediaeval guilds or handicraftsmen and journeymen. We are the representatives of the class interests of the most important, the greatest class of modern society – the working class, to whose destiny it falls to free mankind from the sufferings of the capitalist system, the class which in one sixth of the world has already cast off the yoke of capitalism and constitutes the ruling class. We defend the vital interests of all the exploited, toiling strata, that is, of the overwhelming majority in any capitalist country ...

'The interests of the class struggle of the proletariat against the native exploiters are not in contradiction to the interests of a free and happy future of the nation. On the contrary, the socialist revolution will signify the *salvation of the nation* and will open up to it the road to loftier heights. By the *very fact* of building at the present time its class organizations, by the very fact of defending democratic rights and liberties against fascism, by the very fact of fighting for the overthrow of capitalism, the working class is fighting for the future of the nation'.[55]

The weakening of political ties with the Soviet Union during the war, and the transformation of various Communist Parties into mass organizations which put themselves at the head of national resistance movements against Hitlerism, enabled all the potential implicit in this new line to be proved. But the process of theoretical reformulation did not make the necessary advance and the remnants of class reductionism – streng-

[55] G. Dimitrov, 'The Fascist Offensive and the Tasks of the Communist International'. *Selected Speeches and Articles*, London, 1951.

thened by the second Stalinist ice-age and the Cold War – hung like a millstone and hindered for decades the development of the internal potentialities of this line of ideological and political transformation initiated with the Resistance. A customary misapprehension was the notion that the priority of the democratic struggle thereby determined the progressive character of a sector of the bourgeoisie; to which was counterposed the apparently antagonistic ultra-left thesis that, given the definitively reactionary character of all sectors of the bourgeoisie, it could be concluded that democratic struggles were now obsolete and that it was necessary to confine the struggle to a pure revolutionary class perspective. As we can see, both theses share a class reductionism, since they both consider that democratic ideology can be nothing but bourgeois ideology. If, by contrast, this assumption is abandoned, and it is accepted that popular-democratic ideologies are not class ideologies, the terms of the confrontation are displaced: the basic ideological struggle of the working class consists in linking popular-democratic ideology to its discourse, avoiding both class sectarianism and social-democratic opportunism. This is a difficult balance to keep, but the working class struggle has always been a difficult struggle and has consisted, according to Lenin, in walking between precipices. In this articulation between popular interpellations and proletarian interpellations lies the struggle of the working class for its ideological *hegemony* over the remaining popular sectors.[56] Today, when

[56] The concept of 'hegemony', such as it was defined by Gramsci, is a key concept in Marxist political analysis and one which needs to be developed in all its implications. We cannot go into this analysis on this occasion, but we would like to make the following remarks, based on the interpretation developed by Chantal Mouffe in an unpublished paper of the Gramscian concept of hegemony: (1) The notion of the specific autonomy of democratic interpellations is implicit in the concept of 'hegemony', of democratic ideology as the domain of class struggle and, consequently, it permits Marxist theory to overcome class reductionism. Gramsci's great originality did not lie so much in his insistence in the importance of superstructures in the determination of historical processes – other theoreticians, such as Lukács, had already insisted on this point – but in his effort to overcome *at the same time* economism and class reductionism. Nonetheless, this never led Gramsci to forget that ideological articulations always occur *within* class discourses. As J. M. Piotte asserts: 'The Gramscian concept of hegemony implies therefore two complementary levels: (1) The type of relationship that can win popular masses (2) the class articulation by which the Party organizes its hegemony (predominance of the

the European working class is increasing its influence and must conceive its struggle more and more as a contest for the ideological and political hegemony of middle sectors, it is more necessary than ever for Marxism to develop a rigorous theory of ideological practice which eliminates the last taints of class reductionism. Without this theory the workers' movement will fall into the twin errors of sectarianism and opportunism. The centre of that theory, if the foregoing analysis is correct, must be formed by a theory of the specific autonomy of popular-democratic interpellations.

To rethink and reanalyze the fascist experience seems to me essential for the following reason: fascism has been the extreme form in which popular interpellations in their most radicalized form – jacobinism – could be transformed into the political discourse of the dominant fraction of the bourgeoisie. It is thus a perfect demonstration of the non-class character of popular interpellations. Socialism is not, consequently, the opposite pole of fascism, as it has often tended to be presented – as if fascism were the class ideology of the most conservative and retrograde sectors, along a continuum of liberalism from its right wing to its left-wing versions, culminating in socialism. Socialism is certainly a counterposition to fascism, but in the sense that, whilst fascism was a popular radical discourse, neutralized by the bourgeoisie and transformed by it into its political discourse in a period of crisis, socialism is a popular discourse whose linkage to the radical anti-capitalism of the working class, permits it to develop its full revolutionary potential.

---

proletariat over the peasantry). Certain commentators have overlooked this second level: they gave birth to the different Gramscis, "democratic", or "populist". But the great majority of interpreters have underestimated the importance of the first level: eclipsed by the relationship Lenin-Gramsci, they were unaware of the original and specific traits of Gramscian thought' (*La pensée politique de Gramsci*, Paris, 1970, pp. 129–30). (2) The great themes of Italian Communism that were developed by Togliatti – the mass Party, the progressive democracy, the national tasks of the working class, etc. – would be incomprehensible apart from the idea of hegemony. (3) This idea is nonetheless only sketched and the development of all the *theoretical* implications of the Gramscian concept of hegemony in terms of the non-class character of democratic ideology constitutes to a great extent a task to be accomplished.

4

Towards a Theory of Populism

'Populism' is a concept both elusive and recurrent. Few terms have been so widely used in contemporary political analysis, although few have been defined with less precision. We know intuitively to what we are referring when we call a movement or an ideology populist, but we have the greatest difficulty in translating the intutition into concepts. This has often led to an *ad hoc* kind of practice: the term continues to be used in a merely allusive way and any attempt to ascertain its content is renounced. David Apter, for example, referring to the new political regimes of the Third World, states:

'What we are witnessing in the world today is a range of accommodated political systems. Even the toughest of them is weak. Even the most monolithic in forms tends to be divided in its practices and diluted in its ideas. Few are totalitarian. Almost all are populist and, in a real sense, mainly *pre*democratic rather than *anti*democratic.'[1]

Throughout his book, despite the fact that the 'populism' of these new regimes plays an important role in their characterisation, Apter nowhere seriously tries to determine the content of the concept he uses.

To the obscurity of the concept is linked the indeterminacy of the phenomenon to which it alludes. Is populism a type of movement or a type of ideology? What are its boundaries? In some conceptions it is limited to certain precise social bases; in others, 'populism' indicates a trait common to political phenomena as disparate as Maoism, Nazism, Peronism, Nasserism or Russian *Narodnichestvo.* The result is a vagueness

[1] D. Apter, *The Politics of Modernisation*, London, 1969, p. 2.

which contributes little to a scientific analysis of any political phenomena. The main object of this essay will be to put forward some propositions that may help us to overcome the traditional imprecision. Our objective, then, will be an essentially theoretical one; reference to concrete 'populist' movements will be made only for purposes of illustration. Although the concepts to be employed have been developed basically with Latin American experience in mind, their validity is not limited to a determinate historical or geographical context. We will first discuss various theories of populism, especially functionalist accounts – for these have been the most influential and conceptually refined. We will then present an alternative theoretical schema centred upon the concept of *popular-democratic interpellation*. Finally, we will comment on some characteristics of the historical process experienced by Latin American political systems after 1930, which has made them particularly prone to populist mobilisation.

I

We can single out four basic approaches to an interpretation of populism. Three of them consider it *simultaneously* as a movement and as an ideology. A fourth reduces it to a purely ideological phenomenon.

For the first approach populism is the typical expression of a determinate social class and characterises, therefore, both the movement and its ideology. Populism is deemed to be typical of a distinct social class, whatever the concrete example selected. Thus, for those whose focus of study is 19th century Russian *Narodnichestvo*, populism will be presented essentially as a peasant ideology, or an ideology elaborated by intellectuals that exalts peasant values. If the object of analysis is North American populism, it will be considered an ideology and mobilisation typical of a society of small farmers opposed to urban life and big business. Finally, in Latin America, where the mobilisation of urban masses has often acquired populist connotations, it will be seen as the political and ideological expression either of a petty-bourgeoisie, of marginal sectors, or of a national bourgeoisie seeking to mobilise the masses for a partial confrontation with the local oligarchies and imperialism. The problems of this kind of interpretation are obvious: it evades the phenomenon it sets out to explain. If one is to maintain that there is at least *one* common element between Varguismo, the movement of William Jennings Bryan and *Narodnichestvo*, and that this element is populism, it is obvious that its specificity must be sought *outside*, not within the social bases of those movements, since they are totally dissimilar. If, on the other hand, the use of the concept is restricted to movements with a similar social base, the area of analysis is illegitimately displaced: the object of explanation is now another phenomenon – the 'something in common' present in many different social movements. Yet it was the definition of this specificity which constituted the original problem. As we shall see, this has been typical procedure by which the specificity of populism has been conjured out of existence. The operation is normally carried out in three steps: (1) an initial intuitive perception of populism as constituting a common feature shared by quite distinct political movements, which then determines *a priori* that this feature must find its explanation in the social bases of those movements; (2) concrete populist movements are therefore studied and in the course of research a peculiar transfer of meaning occurs: populism ceases to be considered *a common feature* of various movements and is transformed into a synthetic concept which defines or symbolises the *complex of features* characteristic of the concrete movement under investigation; (3) henceforth, when it is necessary to provide a definition of what is specific about populism, the analyst – rather than isolating a common feature of various movements – is driven to compare these movements *as such* and to try and determine what they have in common via a typically empiricist procedure of abstraction/generalisation. But, as we said, this attempt cannot get very far, since the so-called populist movements differ fundamentally from each other. Consequently what is generally done in such cases, is to continue talking of populism without defining it – which brings us back to our starting point.

The difficulties of establishing the class connotations of populism have often led to a second conception which we might call a kind of theoretical *nihilism*. According to this, 'populism' is a concept devoid of content. It should therefore be eliminated from the vocabulary of the social sciences, and replaced by a direct analysis of the movements which up to now have been called populist – according to their class nature. Hence an analysis of the class bases of any movement is the key to a discovery of its nature. But, we may ask, is that all? Does class analysis really eliminate the problem of populism? It is surely obvious that this is not so. Because at least one unresolved enigma remains: for 'populism' is not just an analytical category but a datum of experience. It is that 'something in common' which is perceived as a component of movements whose social bases are totally divergent. Even if it were a pure illusion or appearance, we would still have to explain the 'illusion' or 'appearance' as such. Peter Worsley has formulated the problem exactly, in the following terms: 'It may well be, then, that to speak of populism as a genus is to assume what needs to be demonstrated: that movements with very different features, separated in time, space and culture, do possess certain crucial attributes which justify our subsuming them consciously and analytically under the same rubric, 'populist', despite variations in their other characteristics. If such a term is to be used, we need to specify just what these crucial attributes are, and not simply assume that the arbitrary bandying about of a word implies any resemblances at all, sociologically speaking, between the activities to which it has become attached. Such resemblances may not exist. But since the word *has* been used, the existence of the verbal smoke might well indicate a fire somewhere.'[2] We can even accept the argument that populism is insufficient to define the concrete specificity of a certain kind of political movement. But can we deny that it constitutes an abstract element of it? These are questions that a mere stance of nihilism cannot answer. Hence the inadequacies of this type of approach. Despite its conceptual indefinition, populism continues to enjoy a good health in the social sciences.

A third conception tries to overcome these difficulties by restricting the term 'populism' to the characterisation of an ideology and not a movement. The typical features of this

[2] P. Worsley, 'The Concept of Populism', in G. Ionescu and E. Gellner, *Populism*, London, 1970, p. 219.

ideology are deemed to be hostility to the status quo, mistrust of traditional politicians, appeal to the people and not to classes, anti-intellectualism, and so on. The ideological complex thus formed can then be adopted by social movements with different bases, according to concrete historical conditions about which it is impossible to formulate any a priori generalisation. But this type of analysis, although it can enrich – in fact has enriched – the study of the *forms* in which populism has appeared, contains two major inadequacies. (1) The characteristic features of populist ideology are presented in a purely descriptive way, that is incapable of constructing their peculiar unity. (2) Nothing is said of the role played by the strictly populist element in a determinate social formation.

Finally, there is the functionalist conception of populism. For the latter, populism is an aberrant phenomenon produced by the asynchronism of the processes of transition from a traditional to an industrial society. The functionalist account is by far the most consistent and developed of all the conceptions we have mentioned so far. In order to discuss it, let us take as an example the well-known model of Gino Germani, together with the derivative analyses of Torcuato Di Tella.

The process of economic development is conceived by Germani,[3] following a well-established sociological tradition, as a transition from a traditional to an industrial society. This transition involves three basic changes: (1) modification of the type of social action: (shift from a predominance of prescriptive to elective actions); (2) passage from an institutionalisation of tradition to that of change; (3) evolution from a relatively undifferentiated complex of institutions to an increasing differentiation and specialisation of them. These three basic changes are accompanied by profound modifications in the predominant type of social relations and personality. (For example, he suggests that modernization of the attitude of children towards parents and wives towards husbands will provoke changes in the attitudes of parents towards children and husbands towards wives. However, these latter attitudes, reflecting the dominant element in the relationship, will not

[3] G. Germani, *Politicay Sociedad en una epoca de transicion*, Buenos Aires, 1965.

necessarily be modern in themselves.) In this model, transitional stages are considered in the form of *asynchronism* – that is to say a coexistence of elements belonging respectively to the two poles of traditional and industrial society. This asynchronism may be *geographical* (dual society; central and peripheral countries or regions); *institutional* (coexistence of institutions corresponding to different phases); *sociological* ('the "objective" characteristics – e.g. occupation, position in the socio-economic structure – and "subjective" characteristics – attitudes, social character, social personality – of certain groups correspond to "advanced" stages, while those of other groups correspond to a "backward" stage'); or *motivational* ('because the same individual belongs to multiple different groups and institutions, asynchronism affects the individual himself. There coexist in his psyche attitudes, ideas, motivations, beliefs corresponding to successive "stages" of the process'). The fit or correspondence between these heterogeneous elements, however, is not reduced to a mere coexistence. The modernisation of one of them will provoke changes in the others, although not necessarily in a modern direction.

Two of these forms of symbiosis appear particularly important to Germani: the *demonstration effect* and the *fusion effect*. In the case of the first, habits and mentalities that correspond to the more advanced stages of developments are diffused in backward areas (such as consumption habits which bear no relation to low levels of production). In the case of the second, ideologies and attitudes corresponding to an advanced stage, on being reinterpreted in a backward context, tend to reinforce traditional features themselves. Two other concepts of key importance in Germani's analysis are those of *mobilisation* and *integration*. By *mobilisation*[4] is understood the process whereby formerly passive groups acquire *deliberative* behaviour (i.e. intervention in national life, which may oscillate between inorganic protest movements and legalised activity channelled through political parties). By *integration* is understood that

[4] The concept of mobilisation has been widely developed in modern political science literature. Cf. especially the works of J. P. Nettl, *Political Mobilisation. A Sociological Analysis of Methods and Concepts*, London, 1967; D. Apter, *op. cit.*; Karl Deutsch 'Social Mobilisation and Political Develooments' in Eckstein and Apter, *Comparative Politics*, New York, 1963, pp. 582–603.

type of mobilisation: (1) which is carried out through existing politico-institutional channels and is thus legalised by the regime in power; (2) in which the regime's framework of legitimacy is implicitly or explicitly accepted by the mobilised groups, such that the rules of the game of the existing legality are accepted.

Using this conceptual system, Germani develops a theoretical framework for an understanding of the emergence of populist movements – or national and popular movements, as he calls them. This theoretical framework is established by a comparison between the historical experience of the transition in Europe and in Latin America. In Europe a clear distinction can be registered between two stages: democracy with limited participation and democracy with total participation. During the first stage the foundations of a rational state with a bureaucratic type of authority are established; there is individual liberty and a liberal State, but political rights are reserved for the bourgeoisie, while popular classes remain shackled to a traditional mentality and unintegrated into the new forms of society; 'capitalist asceticism' predominates, and an ethic of production takes precedence over that of consumption. In the second stage the masses become integrated into political and urban life: but what is important is that this mobilisation occurs by way of a process of integration, which avoids great traumas or profound ruptures in political apparatus of the State. 'The difference between the example of England and other Western countries and the case of Latin America lies, then, in the different degree of correspondence between the gradual mobilisation of an increasing proportion of the population (and eventually all of it) and the emergence of multiple mechanisms of integration – trade-unions, education, social legislation, political parties, mass consumption – capable of absorbing these successive groups, providing them with means for adequate self-expression, both academically and lyrically, as well as other basic aspects of modern culture.'[5] To these changes were added, in European countries, the transition to a new capitalism of big corporations and the predominance of consumer society and the welfare state.

[5] Germani, *op. cit.*, pp. 154.

In present-day underdeveloped societies, and especially in Latin America where Germani concentrates his analysis, the demonstration effect, the fusion effect and asynchronisms far greater than those known in the process of European transition, unite to produce a characteristic political consequence: the impossibility of a *mobilisation* carried out through *integration*. Consequently, mobilisation takes place in aberrant and anti-institutional ways, which constitute the matrix from which emerge the national-popular movements. At the same time the new historical climate of the 20th century, characterised by the decline of liberal democracy and the rise of fascist and communist totalitarianisms, has contributed to this result. 'This is typically reflected in the ideologies of industrialisation, whose essential characteristics seem to be authoritarianism, nationalism and one or other form of socialism, collectivism or state capitalism, that is to say, movements which combine in various ways ideological contents corresponding to opposed political traditions. The result was authoritarianism of the left, nationalism of the left, socialism of the right and a multiplicity of hybrid, even paradoxical, formulas from the point of view of the right-left dichotomy (or continuum). It is precisely these forms, despite their diverse and in many ways opposed variants, that we can subsume beneath the generic label of "national-popular" movements, and which seem to represent the peculiar form of intervention into political life of those strata in the course of rapid mobilisation in countries with delayed industrialisation.'[6]

Germani's explanation of populism, then, boils down to this: the premature incorporation of the masses into Latin American political life created a pressure which went beyond the channels of absorption and participation which the political structures were able to provide. Consequently, mass integration on the model of 19th-century Europe could not be carried out, and various elites, influenced by the new historical climate of the 20th century, manipulated the newly-mobilised masses to serve their own ends. The mentality of these masses, because of their insufficient integration, was characterised by the coexistence of traditional and modern features. Hence popu-

[6] *Op. cit.*, p. 157.

list movements constitute a haphazard accumulation of fragments corresponding to the most dissimilar paradigms. Note the following paragraph of Germani, reminiscent of the 'chaotic enumeration' of surrealist poetry: 'We have here something difficult to understand within the experience of 19th century Europe. Quite different political groups, nationalists of the extreme right, fascists or nazis, stalinist communists, all the variations of trotskyism – and the most diverse sectors – intellectuals, modernised workers, professionals and politicians of petty-bourgeois origin, military men, sectors of the old landowning "oligarchy" in economic and political decline, no less than the most bizarre combinations between them, have tried (sometimes successfully) to base themselves upon this human support in order to achieve their political aims. Obviously, these aims do not always coincide with the aspirations of the mobilised layers themselves, although there can sometimes be an identity of aspirations and objectives between elites and masses.'[7]

A more detailed analysis of populism and its variants, in a similar theoretical perspective to that of Germani, is to be found in a well-known essay by Torcuato di Tella.[8] Populism is defined here as 'a political movement which enjoys the support of the mass of the urban working class and/or peasantry, but which does not result from the autonomous organisational power of either of these two sectors. It is also supported by non-working class sectors upholding an anti-status quo ideology.'[9] In other words, social classes are present in populism but not as classes; a peculiar distortion has separated the *class nature* of these sectors and their forms of political expression. Like Germani, Di Tella associates this distortion with an asynchronism between processes of economic, social and political development. In the case of populism, it is the 'revolution of rising expectations' and the 'demonstration effect' that is responsible for the asynchronism. 'The mass media raise the levels of aspirations of their audience, particularly in the towns and among the educated. This is what has been aptly called

[7] *Op. cit.*, p. 158.
[8] T. Di Tella, 'Populism and Reform in Latin America' in C. Veliz, *Obstacles to Change in Latin America*, London, 1970, pp. 47–74.
[9] *Op. cit.*, p. 47.

the "revolution of rising expectations". . . . Radio, the cinema, the ideals of the Rights of Man, and written constitutions – all tend to produce effects greater than those produced in the European experience. Yet economic expansion lags behind, burdened by demographic explosion, by lack of organisational capacity, by dependence on foreign markets and capital, or by premature efforts at redistribution. A bottleneck necessarily develops, with expectations soaring high above the possibilities of satisfying them.'[10] It is precisely this distortion which makes it impossible for the political system to function in the Western style and consequently leads to the emergence of populism. 'In these conditions, it is difficult for democracy to function properly. In Western experience democracy was traditionally based on the principle of no taxation without representation. In the developing countries, the revolution of rising expectations generates a desire to have representation without ever having been taxed. Groups lacking sufficient economic or organisational national power demand a share in both the goods and decision-making process of society. They no longer "know their place" as European workers knew theirs until recently. They form a disposable mass of supporters, larger and more demanding than any Louis Napoleon would have dreamed of.'[11]

However, a further element is necessary for this mass to be mobilised in a populist direction: the appearance of an élite committed to the process of mobilisation. Di Tella explains the emergence of an élite to lead the populist movement by a new aberrant phenomenon: the existence among these sectors of a status incongruence between aspirations and 'job satisfaction'. The essential features of populism must therefore be sought: (1) in an élite imbued with an anti-status quo ideology; (2) in a mobilised mass generated by a 'revolution of rising expectations'; (3) in an ideology with a widespread emotional appeal. Within this theoretical framework, Di Tella develops a classification of populist movements according to whether or not the leading élite belongs to the upper levels of the social stratification system, and to the degree of acceptance or rejec-

[10] *Op. cit.*, p. 49.
[11] *Op. cit.*, loc. cit.

tion which these élites experience in their groups of origin.

As we can see, Di Tella's conception is as teleological as that of Germani. At one pole is traditional society; at the other, fully developed industrial society. The roots of populism are to be sought in the asynchronism between the processes of transition from one to the other. Populism thus constitutes the form of political expression of popular sectors when they are unable to establish an autonomous organisation and class ideology. To a higher degree of development would correspond more of a 'class' and less of a 'populist' organisation. Peronism, for example, occupies an intermediate position on this continuum. From the point of view of the working class, Western-style trade-unionism would constitute the paradigmatic form of representation of its interests congruent with a highly developed society. (Note that the conception of populism as an aberrant expression of asynchronism in development processes does not necessarily – although frequently it may – imply a negative evaluation of its role in the historical contexts where it appears. Di Tella, for example, considers that populism, although a transitional phenomenon, is an important and positive instrument of reform and change.)

The first objection that the Germani–Di Tella analysis prompts is whether populism can be assigned to a transitional stage of development. Populist experiences have also taken place in 'developed' countries: think of Qualunquismo in Italy or Poujadisme in France, even the Fascist experience, which most conceptions consider as a *sui generis* form of populism. To link populism to a determinate *stage* of development is to make the same mistake as many interpretations in the 1920's – including that of the Comintern – which regarded fascism as an expression of Italy's agrarian underdevelopment, that could not therefore be repeated in advanced industrialised countries such as Germany. It is true that populist experiences in the capitalist metropoles are less frequent than in peripheral countries, but can we therefore conclude that this is due to the different *levels of development* of the two? The argument implies highly questionable assumptions: (1) the greater the level of economic development, the less likelihood of populism; (2) after a certain threshold, when the asynchronisms of the development process have been overcome, industrial societies are immune from the populist phenomenon; (3) 'backward' societies which are today undergoing populist experiences – whether regarded positively or negatively – will necessarily advance towards more 'modern' and 'class' forms of channelling popular protest. These assumptions constitute a set of perfectly arbitrary ideological axioms. What is more, the theory does not provide us with the instruments necessary to ascertain its validity. For the concept of 'industrial society' has not been theoretically constructed – it is the result of an *ad quem* extension of certain features of advanced industrial societies and the simple descriptive addition of those features; while the concept of 'traditional society' is merely the antithesis of each of the features of industrial society taken individually. Within this schema, transitional stages can only consist of the coexistence of features belonging to both poles. Hence 'populist' phenomena can only appear as a confused and motley assortment of 'traditional' and 'modern' characteristics. Hence, too, the appearance of modernising elites appealing to populist mass mobilisation is not satisfactorily explained. (Unless we consider as an explanation what is in reality the reproduction of the problem in different terms – such as the status-incongruence hypothesis; or we accept, with Germani, explanations such as the demonstration effect of the new historical climate created by the crisis of liberal democracy – which appears to be more of an infection than a demonstration effect). Hence, finally, the misuse of explanations in terms of *manipulation*, which either regress to pure moralism (deceit, demagogy) or, in trying to explain what made the 'manipulation' possible, return to the terms of the traditional society/industrial society dichotomy; masses with traditional features are suddenly incorporated into urban life, and so on. The conclusion is unavoidable that in this conception, populism is never defined in itself but only in counterposition to a prior paradigm.

The second criticism to be made of the theory is this. Given that the concepts of the two types of society have not been theoretically constructed but are the result of a simple descriptive addition of their characteristic features, there is no way of understanding the significance of a phenomenon apart from indicating its relative degree of progress: that is, its location on the continuum which leads from traditional society to industrial society. This degree of progress is, in turn, reduced to the respective proportion of 'traditional' and 'modern' elements which enter into the definition of the phenomenon under analysis. Germani would no doubt object that he not only takes into account the presence of isolated elements but also their *functions*, in as much as the bulk of his analysis is devoted *precisely* to studying the particular forms assumed by the combination of elements belonging to the various stages – such as the demonstration and fusion effects – and the real function of those combinations in society as a whole. Let us consider this problem for a moment. In studying the fusion effect, Germani clearly appreciates – and this is certainly a merit – that certain forms of 'modernisation' are not only compatible with but tend to reinforce traditional forms (the modernisation of consumption patterns of traditional oligarchic sectors, for example, can in his analysis contribute to the strengthening of a pre-capitalist consumption ethic and the maintenance of traditional patterns in the sphere of production). So far there would be no objection; indeed, the chosen word, 'fusion' aptly describes the fact that the 'traditional' and 'modern' elements lose their identity as such in the resulting mélange. But if the logic of the case is developed, it comes to negate the premises on which the whole reasoning is based. Let us follow this line of argument: (1) if we accept that the modernisation of certain aspects of society is not necessarily an indicator of the modernisation of that society as a whole – on the contrary, the modernisation of partial aspects can result in a strengthening of a traditional social pattern – we must admit that one society can be more 'traditional' than another from the point of view of some or most of its features, and nevertheless be more 'modern' from the point of view of its structure. This means, on one hand, that the structure cannot be reduced to the mere descriptive addition of its features, and on the other, that the variable relationship between these features and the whole is such that the former, considered in themselves, lack any specific meaning. (2) Henceforth a structural element is introduced into the analysis, from it follows a need to abandon the analysis of transition in terms of a *continuum* of features and attitudes, and to confront it as a *discontinuous* series of structures. (3) Consequently, if the elements considered in isolation lose significance in themselves, to unite them in the paradigms of a 'traditional society' and 'industrial society' is meaningless. Any assertion that the isolated elements have an essence 'in themselves' that is separate from the structures and consists of their insertion into a prior paradigm is a metaphysical statement without legitimacy. It follows that the categories that enable us to conceptualise concrete societies are analytical ones devoid of any historical dimension (if by the latter we are to understand that the notion of stage is present in the very definition of the concept). Consequently, the concepts of *modernisation*, *asynchronism* and in general all those which introduce a teleological perspective into scientific analysis, also lose validity. Germani has incorporated a structural dimension into his analysis with concepts like 'demonstration effect' and 'fusion effect', but he has not taken the consequence of this incorporation to its logical conclusion. For he has retained a teleological approach to the analysis of political phenomena. The elements which 'fuse' are either absolutely 'traditional' or absolutely 'modern'. In what, then, does this process of 'fusion' consist? On this point Germani avoids constructing a concept that would enable us to understand it – 'fusion' is an allusive or metaphorical name, but not a concept – and he substitutes for this construction an explanation in terms of origins: fusion is the result of asynchronism. That is to say, in the fusion effect is only explained what is intelligible within the terms of our two paradigms: the elements which fuse. As generally occurs with explanations in terms of paradigms, all we know at the end of the analysis is what we already knew at the beginning. Paradigms only explain themselves.

Whether or not a teleological perspective and an explanation in terms of paradigms is retained has important consequences for the analysis of concrete political processes. Let us take a common example in the literature on populism: that of the new migrant. This is often cited in order to explain why social sectors coming from backward rural areas, on entering the labour force of newly expanding urban industries, have difficulty in developing European-style trade-unionism and are easily won over by mobilisations of a populist kind. Germani and others tend to explain this phenomenon as essentially the result of two processes: (1) politically inexperienced masses bring with them from rural areas a traditional type of mentality and ideology, which they have not had time to surpass towards a modern ideology and style of political action similar to that of the European working-class; (2) asynchronisms in the development process prematurely throw these masses into political action, whereupon the absence of a developed 'class consciousness' yields deviant forms of mobilisation and does not result in an autonomous organisational activity of the class as such. It is obvious that recently-arrived migrants bring with them a rural type of mentality. It is also obvious that this mentality is transformed in contact with an urban milieu and industrial activity. The problems begin when we try to measure the degree of 'modernity' of these ideologies according to a paradigm constituted by the experience of the European working-class; they are multiplied if we consider that any deviation from this paradigm is an expression of the perpetuation of traditional elements. Let us look at this more closely. Having arrived at an urban centre, the migrant starts to experience a complex of pressures: class exploitation in new places of work, transforming him into a proletarian; multiple pressures of urban society – problems of housing, health, education, through which he enters into a dialectical and conflictual relationship with the State. Under these circumstances, a natural reaction would be to assert the symbols and ideological values of the society from which he has come, in order to express his antagonism towards the new society which exploits him. Superficially this would seem to be the *survival* of old elements, but in reality, behind this survival is concealed a *transformation*: these 'rural elements' are simply the raw materials which the ideological practice of the new migrants transforms in order to express new antagonisms. In this sense, the resistance of certain ideological elements to their articulation in the dominant discourse of older urban sectors *can* express exactly the opposite of traditionalism: a refusal to accept capitalist legality which in this sense – reflecting the most radical of class conflicts – expresses a more 'advanced' and 'modern' attitude than European-style trade unionism. The scientific study of ideologies presupposes precisely the study of this kind of transformation – which consists in a process of articulation and disarticulation of discourses – and of the *ideological terrain* which gives them meaning. But this process is unintelligible so long as ideological elements are pre-assigned to essential paradigms.

The conclusion to be drawn from the foregoing analysis is unequivocal: the meaning of the ideological elements identified with populism must be sought in the structure of which they are a moment, and not in ideal paradigms. These structures seem to refer – again unmistakably – to the class nature of populist movements, to their roots in modes of production and their articulation. Therewith, however, our exploration of theories of populism seems to become circular: we started by pointing out the impossibility of linking the strictly populist element to the *class* nature of a determinate movement; we then analysed theories which present it as the expression of situations in which classes cannot fully express themselves as such; now we conclude that the ideological features which result from these situations only make sense if we refer them to the structures of which they are part, that is to class structures.

II

There would appear to be no way out of a vicious circle. On the one hand, the strictly 'populist' element only finds its specificity if we leave aside consideration of the class nature of concrete populist movements. Yet on the other hand, we must refer to class contradictions as a fundamental structural moment in order to discover the principle of unity of various isolated political and ideological features. However, if we look more closely at the problem, we can see that this vicious circle is in reality the result of a confusion. This confusion arises from a failure to differentiate two aspects: the general problem of *class determination* of political and ideological superstructures, and the *forms of existence* of classes at the level of these superstructures. Note that these are two distinct problems: to assert the class determination of superstructures does not mean establishing the *form* in which this determination is exercised. (Or, to put it in another way, the form in which classes as such are present in them.) To regard these two problems as identical can be justified only if social classes at the ideological and political level are conceived by way of a process of *reduction*. In effect, if every ideological and political element has a *necessary* class belonging, it is obvious that a class is also expressed *necessarily* through each such element; therewith, the political and ideological forms of existence of a class are reduced, as necessary moments, to an unfolding of its essence. Classes then no longer *determine* political and ideological *superstructures*, but *absorb* them as a necessary moment in their process of self-unfolding. This kind of interpretation can, as is well-known, be lent an economist perspective – common in the Marxism of the Second or Third Internationals – that theorizes superstructures as a *reflection* of relations of production, or a 'superstructuralist' perspective (Lukács or Korsch) that makes 'class consciousness' the basic, constitutive moment of class as such. In both cases, however, the relationship between *class* and *superstructure* is conceived in equally reductionist terms. Similarly, this conception leads to an identification between classes as such and empirically observable social groups. Because if every feature of any given group can be reduced – at least in principle – to its class nature, there is no way of distinguishing between the two. The relation between the insertion of the group in the process of production – its class nature – and its 'empirical' features would be of the kind that medieval philosophy established between *natura naturans* and *natura naturata*. It is easy to see, then, why a conception which makes *class reduction* the ultimate source of intelligibility of any phenomenon has met with particular difficulties in the analysis of populism, and has oscillated between reducing it to the expression of class interests – or of the immaturity of a class – and continuing to use the term in an undefined and purely allusive way.

Let us, however, follow a different line of argument. Let us abandon the reductionist assumption and define classes as the poles of antagonistic production relations which have no *necessary*[12] form of existence at the ideological and political levels. Let us assert, at the same time, the determination in the

[12] The conception of ideology and politics as *levels* presents a series of difficulties which we cannot pursue here. We will, continue, therefore, to use the current term.

last instance of historical processes by the relations of production, that is to say, by classes. Three basic consequences follow from this change in emphasis:

(1) *It is no longer possible to think of the existence of classes, at the ideological and political levels, by way of a process of reduction.* If classes are present at the ideological and political levels – since relations of production maintain the role of determination in the last instance – and if the *contents* of ideology and of political practice cease to be the *necessary* forms of existence of classes at these levels, the only way of conceiving this presence is to say that the class character of an ideology is given by its *form* and not by its *content*. What does the form of an ideology consist of? We have seen elsewhere[13] that the answer is in the principle of articulation of its constituent interpellations. The class character of an ideological discourse is revealed in what we could call its *specific articulating principle*. Let us take an example: nationalism. Is it a feudal, bourgeois or proletarian ideology? Considered in itself it has no class connotation. The latter only derives from its specific articulation with other ideological elements. A feudal class, for example, can link nationalism to the maintenance of a hierarchical-authoritarian system of a traditional type – we need only think of Bismarck's Germany. A bourgeois class may link nationalism to the development of a centralised nation-state in fighting against feudal particularism, and at the same time appeal to national unity as a means of neutralising class conflicts – think of the case of France. Finally, a communist movement can denounce the betrayal by capitalist classes of a nationalist cause and articulate nationalism and socialism in a single ideological discourse – think of Mao, for example. One could say that we understand by nationalism something distinct in the three cases. This is true, but our aim is precisely to determine where this difference lies. Is it the case that nationalism refers to such diverse contents that it is not possible to find a common element of meaning in them all? Or rather is it that certain common nuclei of meaning are connotatively linked to diverse ideological-articulatory domains? If the first solution were accepted, we would have to conclude that

[13] cf. supra pp. 101–102.

ideological struggle as such is impossible, since classes can only compete at the ideological level if there exists a common framework of meaning shared by all forces in struggle. It is precisely this background of shared meanings that enables antagonistic discourses to establish their difference. The political discourses of various classes, for example, will consist of antagonistic efforts of articulation in which each class presents itself as the authentic representative of 'the people', of 'the national interest', and so on. If, therefore, the second solution – which we consider to be the correct answer – is accepted, it is necessary to conclude that *classes exist at the ideological and political level in a process of articulation and not of reduction.*

(2) Articulation requires, therefore, the existence of non-class contents[14] – interpellations and contradictions – which constitute the raw material on which class ideological practices operate. These ideological practices are determined not only by a view of the world consistent with the insertion of a given class in the process of production, but also by its relations with other classes and by the actual level of class struggle. The ideology of a dominant class does not merely consist of a Weltanschauung which ideologically expresses its essence, but is a functioning part of the system of rule of that class. The ideology of the dominant class, *precisely because it is dominant*, interpellates not only the members of that class but also members of the dominated classes. The concrete form in which the interpellation of the latter takes place is a partial absorption and neutralisation of those ideological contents through which resistance to the domination of the former is expressed. The characteristic method of securing this objective is to eliminate antagonism and transform it into a simple difference. A class is hegemonic not so much to the extent that it is able to impose a uniform conception of the world on the rest of society, but to the extent that it can articulate different visions of the world in such a way that their potential antagonism is neutralised. The English bourgeoisie of the 19th century was transformed into a hegemonic class not through the imposition of a uniform ideology upon other classes, but to the extent that it succeeded in articulating different ideologies to its hege-

[14] Practices are of course always embodied in ideological apparatuses.

monic project by an elimination of their antagonistic character: the aristocracy was not abolished, in the jacobin style, but was reduced to an increasingly subordinate and decorative role, while the demands of the working class were partially absorbed – which resulted in reformism and trade-unionism. The particularism and *ad hoc* nature of dominant institutions and ideology in Great Britain does not, therefore, reflect an inadequate bourgeois development but exactly the opposite: the supreme articulating power of the bourgeoisie[15]. Similarly, ideologies of dominated classes consist of articulating projects which try to develop the potential antagonisms constituting a determinate social formation. What is important here is that the dominant class exerts its hegemony in two ways: (1) through the articulation into its class discourse of non-class contradictions and interpellations; (2) through the absorption of contents forming part of the ideological and political discourses of the dominated classes. The presence of working-class demands in a discourse – the eight-hour day, for example – is insufficient to determine the class nature of that discourse. The political discourse of the bourgeoisie also came to accept the eight-hour day as a 'just' demand, and to adopt advanced social legislation. This is a clear proof that it is not in the presence of determinate *contents* of a discourse but in the articulating principle which unifies them that we must seek the class character of politics and ideology.

Can a dominant class, through the successive accumulation of elements from ideological discourses of dominated classes, reach a point at which its very class articulating principles are called into question? This is the thesis argued by C. B. Macpherson, for example. He wrote of the dilemmas of liberal-democratic theory in the 20th century, that 'It must continue to use the assumptions of possessive individualism, at a time when the structure of market society no longer provides the necessary conditions for deducing a valid theory of political obligation from those assumptions'.[16] Class struggle determines changes

[15] On this point we disagree with Perry Anderson's view that the persistence of British institutional and ideological particularism is the expression of an incompletely consummated bourgeois revolution. Cf. Perry Anderson, 'Origins of the Present Crisis', *New Left Review*, No. 23.

[16] C. B. Macpherson, *The Political Theory of Possessive Individualism*,

in the ideological-articulating capacity of classes. When a dominant class has gone too far in its absorption of contents of the ideological discourse of the dominated classes, it runs the risk that a crisis may reduce its own neutralising capacity and that the dominated classes may impose their own articulating discourse within the State apparatus. That is today the case in Western Europe, where the expansion of monopoly capital is becoming more and more contradictory to the liberal democratic institutions created by the bourgeoisie in its competitive stage, and where consequently the defence and extension of democratic liberties are becoming more and more linked to an alternative socialist discourse. Another more classic example, is the transformation, described by Lenin, of democratic banners into socialist banners in the course of a revolutionary process.

(3) The third conclusion that follows from the analysis is that if classes are defined as the antagonistic poles of a mode of production, and if the relation between the levels of production and the levels of political and ideological superstructures must be conceived in the form of articulation and not of reduction, classes and empirically observable groups do not necessarily coincide. Individuals are the bearers and points of intersection of an accumulation of contradictions, not all of which are class contradictions. From this follows: (a) although class contradictions take priority in this accumulation of contradictions, and although any other contradiction exists articulated to class discourses, it cannot be concluded – since we have eliminated the reductionist assumption – that the class which articulates these other contradictions is necessarily the class to which the individual belongs. This is the phenomenon of 'alienation' or 'false consciousness' – terms with which subjectivist theories have tried to explain the ideological colonisation of one class by another and which, since they assigned a class belonging to every ideological element, they could only conceive as a collapse or an inadequate development of 'class consciousness'. Within our theoretical framework, on the contrary, this kind of phenomenon would correspond to those situations where the non-

---

Oxford, 1972, p. 275.

class interpellations and contradictions in which the individual participates are subjected to the articulating principle of a class distinct from that to which the individual belongs. (b) If classes constitute themselves as such at the level of production relations, and if the articulating principle of a discourse is always a class principle, it follows that those sectors – such as the middle classes – which do not participate in the relations of production that are basic to a society, will lack an articulating principle of their own and the unification of their ideology will depend on other classes. They can never constitute themselves, therefore, as hegemonic classes. (c) If the hegemony of a class consists in the articulation into its own discourse of non-class interpellations, and if classes only exist at the political and ideological level as articulating principles, it follows that a class only exists as such as those levels to the extent that it struggles for its hegemony.[17]

It follows from the previous analysis that it is possible to assert the class belonging of a movement or an ideology and, at the same time, to assert the non-class character of some of the interpellations which constitute it. At this point we can start to perceive where the enigma of 'populism' lies and to glimpse a possible way out of the vicious circle into which analysis of various theories of populism led us. If we can prove that the strictly 'populist' element does not lie in the movement as such, nor in its characteristic ideological discourse – for these always have a class belonging – but in a specific non-class contradiction articulated into that discourse, we will have resolved the apparent paradox. Our next task, therefore, must be to determine whether or not this contradiction exists.

Let us begin by asking if there is a common nucleus of meaning in all the uses to which the term 'populism' has been put. It is evident that the term is ambiguous, but the problem is to determine what kind of ambiguity. Aristotle distinguished between three kinds of terms: those which only permitted one meaning he called *univocal*; those which admitted two meanings but with no relation between them apart from the verbal unity of the name he called *equivocal*; finally, he called *analogical* those terms which have quite distinct meanings, but in

[17] For the concept of heremony see supra p. 141, footnote 56.

which we can find reference to a common element which constitutes the analogic basis of all possible uses of the term (for example, 'healthy', which can be applied to a person, a walk, a climate, a meal, but which throughout its different uses retains a common reference to *health* – which is thus the analogical basis of all the possible uses of the term 'healthy'). Now, is the ambiguity we observe in the term 'populism', equivocal or analogical? The answer must be that it is the second, because despite the wide diversity in the uses of the term, we find in all of them the common reference to an analogical basis which is *the people.* According to a widely-known theory, populism is characterised by its appeal to the people above class divisions. This definition fails both by excess and by default: by default, since a populist discourse can refer *both* to the people *and* to classes (presenting, for example, a class as the historical agent of the people's interests); and by excess since, as we will see, not all reference to 'the people' automatically transforms a discourse into a 'populist' one. But in any case, it is certainly true that reference to 'the people' occupies a central place in populism. This is where we find the basic source of the ambiguity surrounding 'populism': *the people* is a concept without a defined theoretical status; despite the frequency with which it is used in political discourse, its conceptual precision goes no further than the purely allusive or metaphorical level. We said at the outset of this essay that 'populism' is both an elusive and a recurrent concept. Now we understand why it is elusive: all the uses of the term refer to an analogical basis which, in turn, lacks conceptual precision. The recurrence of the term remains to be explained. Some light may be thrown on why it continues to be used, if we could show that the notion of 'the people' is linked to a specific contradiction which, although not theoretically defined, is of decisive importance in the analysis of any political conjuncture.

This is the point at which our previous analysis may clarify matters. As we have seen,[18] 'the people' is not merely a rhetorical concept but an objective determination, one of the two poles of the dominant contradiction at the level of a concrete

[18] cf. supra, p. 108.

social formation. Let us recall the main conclusions of our analysis: (1) the 'people'/power bloc contradiction is an antagonism whose intelligibility depends not on the relations of production but the complex of political and ideological relations of domination constituting a determinate social formation; (2) if the dominant contradiction at the level of the mode of production constitutes the specific domain of class struggle, the dominant contradiction at the level of a concrete social formation constitutes the specific domain of the popular-democratic struggle; (3) however, as class struggle takes priority over popular-democratic struggle, the latter only exists articulated with class projects. But, in turn, as political and ideological class struggle takes place on a terrain constituted by non-class interpellations and contradictions, this struggle can only consist of antagonistic projects for the articulation of those non-class interpellations and contradictions.

This perspective opens up the possibility for understanding a phenomenon which has not received an adequate explanation in Marxist theory: *the relative continuity* of popular traditions, in contrast to the historical discontinuities which characterise class structures. Marxist political discourse – like any radical popular discourse – abounds in references to 'the secular struggle of the people against oppression', 'popular traditions of struggle', to the working class as 'the agent of uncompleted popular tasks', and so on. As we know, these traditions are crystallised in symbols or values in which the subjects interpellated by them find a principle of identity. One could say that we have here symbols of merely emotional value and that appeal to them has only a rhetorical significance. But this kind of explanation – apart from not making clear why the emotional appeal is effective – does not succeed in resolving a real dilemma. If we accept the universality of the class criterion, and at the same time speak of the *secular* struggle of the people against oppression, the ideology in which that secular struggle is crystallised can only be that of a class other than the working-class – since the latter only arises with modern industrialism. But in that case, the appeal to this tradition in socialist discourse would constitute crass opportunism, since it taints the ideological purity of proletarian ideology with the injection of ideological elements characteristic of other classes. If we take the opposite course and accept that these traditions do not constitute class ideologies, we are confronted with the problem of determining their nature. The theoretical perspective previously outlined enables us to overcome this impasse. 'Popular traditions' constitute the complex of interpellations which express the 'people'/power bloc contradiction as distinct from a class contradiction. This enables us to explain two things. In the first place, in so far as 'popular traditions' represent the ideological crystallisation of resistance to oppression in general, that is, *to the very form of the State*, they will be longer lasting than class ideologies and will constitute a structural frame of reference of greater stability. But in the second place, popular traditions do not constitute consistent and organised discourses but merely *elements* which can only exist in articulation with class discourses. This explains why the most divergent political movements appeal to the same ideological symbols. The figure of Tupac Amaru can be evoked by various guerrilla movements and by the present military government in Peru; the symbols of Chinese nationalism were conjured up by Chiang-Kai-Shek and by Mao Tse Tung; those of German nationalism by Hitler and by Thälmann. But even though they constitute mere elements, popular traditions are far from being arbitrary and they cannot be modified at will. They are the residue of a unique and irreducible historical experience and, as such, constitute a more solid and durable structure of meanings than the social structure itself. This dual reference to the people and to classes constitutes what we could call the *double articulation of political discourse*.

Let us take a particularly illustrative example: the recent and excellent analysis of Engels's *Peasant Wars in Germany* by Alain Badiou and François Balmès. These two authors arrive at conclusions similar to ours in some respects, albeit from a theoretical and political perspective with which I am far from concurring. As they point out, Engels' text constitutes a perfect example in which we can see the limits of a mere class analysis. Engels says: 'At that time [XVth and early XVIth century] the plebeians were the only class that stood outside

[19] F. Engels, *The Peasant Wars in Germany*, Moscow 1956, pp. 59–60.

the existing official society. . . . They had neither privileges nor property: they did not even have the kind of property the peasant or petty burgher had, weighed down as it was with burdensome taxes. They were unpropertied and rightless in every respect; their living conditions never even brought them into direct contact with the existing institutions, which ignored them completely. . . . This explains why the plebeian opposition even then could not stop at fighting only feudalism and the privileged burghers; why, in fantasy at least, it reached beyond the then scarcely dawning modern bourgeois society; why, an absolutely propertyless faction, it questioned the institutions, views and conceptions common to all societies based on class antagonisms. . . . The anticipation of communism nurtured by fantasy became in reality an anticipation of modern bourgeois conditions. . . . Only in the teachings of Münzer did these Communist notions express the aspirations of a real fraction of society. It was he who formulated them with a certain definiteness, and they are since observed in every great popular upheaval, until they gradually merge with the modern proletarian movement.' The terms of the problem are clear. We find in Münzer a Communist programme which will persist as an ideological theme in all the great popular uprisings of the mercantilist epoch, until they fuse with the programme of the modern proletariat. (Engels goes as far as to assert that the communist sects of the 19th century, on the eve of the March revolution, were no better equipped theoretically than the followers of Münzer). The problem, as Badiou and Balmès point out, is to determine the class practice of which this programme was an expression. Engels's answer on this point is hesitant. On one hand he tries to resolve the problem within a strictly class framework: a communist programme can only be the programme of the proletariat, and in that sense, the Münzerite plebeians of the 16th century were an embryonic proletariat which expressed itself ideologically through a kind of mass communism. But, according to Badiou and Balmès, this is not a convincing response, since all the evidence shows that this was a communist ideology which reflected and unified a peasant revolt. Peasant insurrections generate ideas of an egalitarian and communist kind, and it was these ideas which Thomas Münzer systematised. Consequently, it is necessary to favour an alternative solution. Basing themselves on other passages of the same text of Engels, Badiou and Balmès suggest the following: '"Communist resonances" are a constant in popular uprisings, partially autonomous from the "modern proletarian movement" which is the historical agent of them. Here in the ideological sphere is opened up a dialectic between *the people* and the *proletariat*, to which Maoism has given its fullest expression.'[20] Badiou and Balmès then derive the following theoretical conclusions: 'All the great mass revolts of successive exploited classes (slaves, peasants, proletarians) have as their ideological expression egalitarian, anti-property and anti-state formulations which form the features of a communist programme. . . . These elements of the general position taken by insurgent producers we call *communist constants*: ideological constants of a communist kind, continually regenerated by the process of unification of great popular revolts at all times. Communist constants do not have a defined class character: they synthesise the universal aspiration of the exploited, which is to overthrow the whole principle of exploitation and oppression. *They come into existence on the terrain of the contradiction between masses and the State.* Naturally, this contradiction is itself structured in class terms, for the State is always that of a particular dominant class. However, there is a general form of the State, organically linked to the very existence of classes and of exploitation, and it is against this that the masses invariably arise, as bearers of its dissolution and of the historic movement which "will relegate the whole apparatus of the State where it will henceforward belong in the museum of antiquities, along with the spinning-wheel and the bronze axe".'

This analysis has the indubitable merit of isolating 'the people' as the pole of a contradiction which is not that of class, and of positing this contradiction as the opposition of the masses to the State. The difficulty with the formulation of Badiou and Balmès, however, is that it confuses the form of logical resolution of the contradiction they analyse – that is,

[20] A. Badiou et F. Balmès, *De l'Idéologie,* Paris, 1976, p. 66.
[21] *Op. cit.* p. 67.

the suppression of the State – with the concrete and historical forms of existence of that contradiction. Neither of the two terms of what they call 'communist constants' can be justified without qualification. Communism does not represent the normal form of existence of an 'egalitarian, anti-property and anti-state' ideology of the masses, but a particular articulation of it: that which precisely permits the development of all the potential antagonism of that ideology. Normally, the antagonism inherent in this contradiction is neutralised and partially absorbed in the discourse of the dominant classes. Macpherson, for example, has studied the way in which popular-democratic ideology was progressively separated from those antagonistic elements which at the beginning of the 19th century were identified with government by 'underlings' and with a hated jacobinism, such that it could be absorbed and neutralised by dominant liberal ideology. He comments: 'By the time democracy came, in the present liberal-democratic countries, it was no longer opposed to the liberal society and the liberal state. It was, by then, not an attempt by the lower classes to overthrow the liberal state or the competitive market economy; it was an attempt by the lower class to take their fully and fairly competitive place within those institutions and that system of society. Democracy had been transformed. From a threat to the liberal state it had become a fulfilment of the liberal state. . . . The liberal state fulfilled its own logic. In so doing, it neither destroyed nor weakened itself; it strengthened both itself and the market society. It liberalised democracy while democratising liberalism.'[22]

Just as popular-democratic ideology could be articulated with liberalism, so it can be articulated also with socialism and other class ideologies. In his book, Macpherson studies some of these articulations. The conclusion is clear: democracy only exists at the ideological level in the form of elements of a discourse. There is no popular-democratic discourse as such. In this sense, democracy is not spontaneously communist for the simple reason that there is no democratic spontaneity. Popular-democratic struggle is subordinate to class struggle and democratic ideology only exists articulated as an abstract

[22] C. B. Macpherson, *The Real World of Democracy*, Oxford, 1975, pp. 10–11.

moment in a class discourse. I think that it is necessary to establish a distinction here: (1) *spontaneous* mass ideology, articulated as a whole, will always be a class ideology; (2) however, democratic ideological elements can *potentially* lead to communism to the extent that the logical development of the 'people'/power bloc contradiction leads to the suppression of the State. But the antagonistic potentialities of a contradiction and its actual form of existence – which is what spontaneity consists of – are very different. The transformation of the antagonistic potential of democracy into concrete mass spontaneity depends on a historical condition which goes beyond the domain of popular-democratic struggle: on the rise *as a hegemonic force* of a class whose own interests carry it to a suppression of the State. In that sense, only socialism represents the possibility of full development and supersession of the 'people'/power bloc contradiction.

This may help us see why it is mistaken to call popular ideologies *constants*.[23] If we are referring to ideologies articulated as a whole, it is obvious that they are not 'constants' but that they change according to the rhythm of the class struggle. If we refer, on the other hand, to the popular-democratic elements of a discourse, the transformation process is more complex but, in any case, we still cannot talk of constants. Let us take an example to illustrate our argument. Let us imagine a semi-colonial social formation in which a dominant fraction of landowners exploits indigenous peasant communities. The ideology of the dominant bloc is liberal and Europeanist, while that of the exploited peasantry is anti-European, indigenist and communitarian. This second ideology – the sole opponent of the power bloc – has therefore, a clear peasant origin. In that society develops a growing urban opposition of middle- and working-classes who challenge the hegemonic landowning fraction's monopoly of power. In these circumstances, the organic intellectuals of these new groups, trying to make their political opposition consistent and systematic, increasingly appeal to the symbols and values of peasant groups,

[23] Badiou and Balmès might object that they do not call popular ideologies themselves constants, only the communist elements in them. This does not affect our criticism, however, because as we have argued, communism is not a constant but one of the possible articulations of popular-democratic elements.

because they constitute the only ideological raw materials which, in this social formation, express a radical confrontation with the power bloc. But in the urban reformulation of those symbols and values, they become transformed: they lose their reference to a concrete social base and are transformed into the ideological expression of the 'people'/power bloc confrontation. Henceforth they have lost all class reference and can, therefore, be articulated into the ideological discourses of the most divergent classes. What is more, no political discourse can do without them: dominant classes to neutralise them, dominated classes to develop their potential antagonism, these ideological elements are always present in the most varied articulations. (Think of the metamorphoses of Mexican nationalism, of the omnipresence of indigenism as an ideological symbol in Peru, or of the opposing reformulations of the ideological symbols of Peronism by its left and right fractions). This explains why these ideological elements *qua* elements change more slowly than the class structure: because they represent simple abstract moments of a discourse and express a contradiction inherent in any class society, which is not linked exclusively to a determinate mode of production. But, as we have seen, they also become transformed, even though they move more slowly and obey different laws from those which govern class discourses.

We have, then, determined the theoretical status of the concept of 'the people' and the specific contradiction of which it constitutes a pole. However, we still have not defined the specificity of populism. Can we consider as populist that type of discourse where popular-democratic interpellations predominate? Obviously not. Numerous ideological discourses make reference to 'the people' which we would not think of calling 'populist'. If, therefore, it is not the mere *presence* of popular-democratic interpellations in a discourse which transforms it into a species populism and if, however, we know that populism is directly linked to the presence of 'the people' in this discourse, we must conclude that what transforms an ideological discourse into a populist one is *a peculiar form of articulation of the* popular-democratic interpellations in it. *Our thesis is that populism consists in the presentation of popular-democratic interpellations as a synthetic-antagonistic complex with respect to the dominant ideology.* Let us look at this in detail. As we have seen, the ideology of dominant classes not only interpellates dominant subjects but also dominated classes, with the effect of neutralising their potential antagonism. As we have also said, the basic method of this neutralisation lies in a transformation of all antagonism into simple difference. The articulation of popular-democratic ideologies within the dominant discourse consists in an absorption of everything in it which is a simple differential particularity and a repression of those elements which tend to transform the particularity into a symbol of antagonism. (The clientelism of rural districts, for example, exalts everything that is folklore in mass ideology, at the same time as it presents the *caudillo* as the intermediary between the masses and the State, tending to suppress the antagonistic elements in it.) It is in this sense that the presence of popular elements in a discourse is not sufficient to transform it into a populist one. Populism starts at the point where popular-democratic elements are presented as an antagonistic option against the ideology of the dominant bloc. Note that this does not mean that populism is *always* revolutionary. It is sufficient for a class or class fraction to need a substantial transformation in the power bloc in order to assert its hegemony, for a populist experience to be possible. We can indicate in this sense a populism of the dominant classes and a populism of the dominated classes:

(a) When the dominant bloc experiences a profound crisis because a new fraction seeks to impose its hegemony but is unable to do so within the existing structure of the power bloc, one solution can be a direct appeal by this fraction to the masses to develop their antagonism towards the State. As I have pointed out elsewhere,[24] this was the case with Nazism. Monopoly capital could not impose its hegemony within the existing institutional system – as it had done in England or France – nor could it base itself on the army which constituted an enclave under the feudal influence of the Junkers. The only solution was a mass movement which would develop the potential antagonism of popular interpellations, but articulated in a way which would obstruct its orientation in any

[24] Cf. supra, p. 119.

revolutionary direction. Nazism constituted a populist experience which, like any populism of the dominant classes, had to appeal to a set of ideological distortions – racism, for example – to avoid the revolutionary potential of popular interpellations from being reoriented towards their true objectives. The populism of the dominant classes is always highly repressive because it attempts a more dangerous experience than an existing parliamentary regime: whilst the second simply *neutralises* the revolutionary potential of popular interpellations, the first tries to *develop* that antagonism but to keep it within certain limits.

(b) For the dominated sectors, ideological struggle consists in an expansion of the antagonism implicit in democratic interpellations and in an articulation of it with their own class discourses. The struggle of the working class for its hegemony is an effort to achieve the maximum possible fusion between popular-democratic ideology and socialist ideology. In this sense a 'socialist populism' is not the most backward form of working class ideology but the most advanced – the moment when the working class has succeeded in condensing the ensemble of democratic ideology in a determinate social formation within its own ideology. Hence the unequivocally 'populist' character adopted by victorious socialist movements: think of Mao, think of Tito, and think even of the Italian Communist Party – which has come the closest in Western Europe to a hegemonic position – and has frequently been called populist.

So we see why it is possible to call Hitler, Mao and Peron simultaneously populist. Not because the social bases of their movements were similar; not because their ideologies expressed the same class interests but because popular interpellations appear in the ideological discourses of all of them, presented in the form of antagonism and not just of difference. Opposition to dominant ideology may be more or less radical, and therefore the antagonism will be articulated in the discourses of the most divergent classes, but in any case it is always present, and this presence is what we intuitively perceive as the specifically populist element in the ideology of the three movements.

Finally, let us recall what our study of fascism remarked of *Jacobinism.* After indicating the way in which popular interpellations are articulated into discourses of a clientelist type and in those of popular parties, we pointed out that in Jacobinism the autonomy of popular-democratic interpellations reaches its maximum degree compatible with a class society. We also said that this was only a transitory moment which, sooner or later, must dissolve with the reabsorption of popular interpellations by class ideological discourses. What is important is that this reabsorption can be effected in two ways: either the popular-democratic elements are kept at the level of *mere* elements in so far as the existing ideological framework is increasingly accepted, or a crystallisation of the Jacobin inflexion occurs – an organisation of popular-democratic interpellations into a synthetic totality which, united with other interpellations which adapt Jacobinism to the interests of the classes which express themselves through it, presents itself as an antagonist of the existing ideological framework. The first solution signifies a reconversion of the phase of *Jacobinism* to the phase of *popular parties*. The second solution is populism. It is clear, then: (1) that what is populist in an ideology is the presence of popular-democratic interpellations in their specific antagonism; (2) that the ideological complex of which populism is a moment consists in the articulation of this antagonistic moment within divergent class discourses. It cannot therefore be said that concrete populist ideologies are above classes, but neither can the strictly populist moment be linked to the discourse of a determinate social class.

If the argument so far is correct, the emergence of populism is historically linked to a crisis of the dominant ideological discourse which is in turn part of a more general social crisis. This crisis can either be the result of a fracture in the power bloc, in which a class or class fraction needs, in order to assert its hegemony, to appeal to 'the people' against established ideology as a whole; or of a crisis in the ability of the system to neutralise the dominated sectors – that is to say, a crisis of transformism. Naturally, an important historical crisis combines both ingredients. What should be clear, however, is that the 'causes' of populism have little to do with a determinate *stage of development*, as functionalist theses suppose. It is true that the long process of expansion of the forces of production which characterised Europe in the stage of monopoly capitalism increased the system's ability to absorb and neutralise its contradictions. But it is also true that each time the capitalist system has experienced a serious crisis in Western Europe, various forms of populism have flourished. We need only think of the crisis after the First World War which produced the triumph of fascism, the world economic crisis which led to the ascent of Nazism, and the world recession today that is accompanied by the multiplication of regionalisms that tend to be expressed in ideologies which make of populism a central moment.

III

Let us take, as an example of a populist articulation of democratic interpellations, a case which is particularly illustrative because of the multiple metamorphoses which it underwent: Peronism. No other Latin American populist movement was constituted from the articulation of more disparate interpellations; no other achieved such success in its attempt to transform itself into the common denominator of mass popular-democratic language; no other, finally, was articulated into such varied class discourses.

Peronism – together with Varguism – has been considered one of the two typical examples of a Latin American populist movement. From the previous argument we may deduce that this expression – 'populist movements' – contains an ambiguity which needs clarification. It is certainly inexact if we wish to characterise the nature of those movements, but it is correct if we use it to allude to the presence of 'populism' as a moment in their ideological structure. An ideology is not 'populist' in the same sense that it is 'conservative', 'liberal' or 'socialist', for the simple reason that, whilst these three terms allude to the articulating principles of the respective ideologies considered as a whole, 'populism' alludes to a kind of contradiction which only exists as an abstract moment of an ideological discourse. Hence the problem of the reasons for the proliferation of populist movements in Latin America after 1930 can be more exactly reformulated in the following terms: why did the ideological discourses of political movements with quite distinct orientations and social bases have to have increasing recourse to populism, that is to say, to develop the potential antagonism of popular-democratic interpellations?

A fairly generalised opinion tends to link 'populism' with import substitution industrialisation. Francisco Weffort and Octavio Ianni[25] have produced the best studies of Latin American populism from this perspective. It follows from what has been said that we cannot share this criterion: 'populism' is not the *necessary* superstructure of any social or economic process. Populist phenomena can present themselves in the most varied contexts to the extent that certain conditions for them are met. If, therefore, we try to explain why movements with populist ideologies flourished in Latin America between 1930 and 1960, this explanation must show how the conditions necessary for the emergence of populist phenomena were united in this period and were, on the other hand, much less frequent before and after it. We have already established what these conditions are: a particularly serious crisis of the power bloc which results in a fraction of it seeking to establish its hegemony through mass mobilisation, and a crisis of transformism.

To understand the specificity of the populist rupture, from which Peronism emerged, it is necessary to understand the nature of the previous dominant ideological system in Argentina, and its characteristic articulating principles. We must note two things in this respect: (a) that the principle of unity of an ideological discourse is provided not by the development of the logical implications of a determinate interpellation but by the power of condensation it has in a specific connotative domain; (b) that class hegemony consists not only in an ability to impose a 'conception of the world' upon other classes, but also, and especially, in an ability to articulate different 'conceptions of the world' in such a way as to neutralise their potential antagonism.

In Argentina before the crisis of 1930, the hegemonic class in the power bloc was the landowning oligarchy, and the basic articulating principle of its ideological discourse was liberal-

[25] Cf. especially F. Weffort, 'Clases sociales y desarrollo social (Contribución al estudio del populismo)' in A. Quijano y F. Weffort, *Populismo, marginalidad y dependencia*, Costa Rica, 1973; O. Ianni, *La Formación del Estado populista en America Latina*, Mexico, 1975.

ism. The reasons for this are to be found in a double circumstance common to all Latin America from the mid-19th century to 1930: if on the one hand the full incorporation of the Latin American economies into the world market necessitated the constitution of nation-states, which created the conditions of political stability and institutional continuity necessary for economic activity to develop, on the other hand, political power remained in the hands of local landowning oligarchies. Now if in Europe these two constellations were contradictory – since the liberal state arose largely in the struggle against feudal particularism – in Latin America they were complementary, since it was the landowning oligarchies who were seeking to maximise their production for the world market and who, therefore, sought to organise a central State. The emergent Latin American political systems sought to give expression to this dual situation: centralised states were formed in which the representation of local oligarchical interests predominated. The formula most adapted to this situation was a parliamentary liberal state with a strong predominance of the Legislative over the Executive. The degree of decentralisation of power varied greatly in the different Latin American countries. In some cases the Executive was reduced to a mere arbitrator – think of the old Republic in Brazil or of the constitutional reorganisation of Chile after the revolution of 1891. In other cases, like Argentina, where the ensemble of power and wealth was concentrated in a relatively limited area of territory, the decentralisation was less and the Executive enjoyed greater autonomy. But in all cases, whatever the form, the central state was conceived as a federation of local oligarchies. Parliamentary power and landowning hegemony became synonymous in Latin America.

The very historical process of the implantation and consolidation of the oligarchic state in Argentina explains the specific connotative domain with which liberal ideology was articulated. *In the first place*, liberalism initially had little ability to absorb the democratic ideology of the masses and integrate it into its discourse. Democracy and liberalism were opposed to each other. Imperialist penetration and the incorporation of the country into the world market in the second half of the 19th century necessitated the dissolution of previous forms of social organisation and precapitalist relations of production. This involved a violent and repressive policy towards the dominated classes. The struggles between the interior of the country and Buenos Aires, the Montonero Rebellion of the 1860's, the uprising of Lopez Jordan in the early 1870's, were episodes in this struggle through which the liberal state was imposed. *In the second place*, liberalism was throughout this period connotatively articulated to economic development and material progress as positive ideological values. (Note that this is not a necessary articulation: after 1930 liberalism and developmental ideology were definitively to lose any capacity for mutual implication). *In the third place*, liberal ideology was articulated to 'Europeanism', that is to say, to a defence of the European way of life and ideological values as representing 'civilisation'. There was a radical rejection of popular national traditions, considered to be synonymous with backwardness, obscurantism and stagnation. *In the fourth place*, Argentinian liberalism was consequently anti-personalist. The emergence of national political leaders with direct contact to the masses, which could take precedence over the local political machines with their clientelistic base, was always viewed with mistrust by oligarchic power.

These four ideological elements, of which liberalism was the articulating principle, constituted the system of coordinates defining the ideological domain of oligarchic hegemony. Positivism was the philosophical influence which systematised these distinct elements into a homogeneous whole. Popular ideologies – that is to say, that complex of interpellations constituting popular subjects in their opposition to the power bloc – exhibited the opposite features. It was therefore natural for popular resistance to be expressed in anti-liberal ideologies; for it to be nationalist and anti-European; for it to defend popular traditions against the corrosive effects of capitalist expansion; for it to be, therefore, *personalist* and to lend support to popular leaders who represented a politics hostile to the status quo. How were the ideological symbols of this popular resistance elaborated? As we have already said, ideological practice always works with raw materials constituted by prior interpellations which, on being disarticulated from the class discourses into which they were formerly integrated, lose any necessary class belonging. In the Andean countries popular resistance was increasingly expressed through indigenist symbols, which originally represented the resistance to the dissolution of peasant communities but which, reinterpreted by urban sectors, lost any necessary rural connotation and came to be symbols of popular resistance in general. In Argentina, by contrast, where there were no peasant traditions and where massive immigration had radically modified the social structure of the country, anti-liberal popular resistance utilized the traditions of the 19th century Montoneros, the ideological symbols of the federalism that had opposed the Europeanizing unitarism of Buenos Aires.[26]

The problem is then: to what extent did the dominant oligarchic bloc during this period succeed in neutralising its contradictions with 'the people' and in articulating popular-democratic interpellations into liberal discourse? This is exactly the problem discussed by Macpherson, as we mentioned before: to what extent was democracy liberalised and liberalism democratised? To what extent was the ideological discourse of the dominated classes neutralised and its protest maintained at the stage of *popular parties*, and to what extent did it become jacobinised and lead to populism?

The answer to this question leaves no room for doubt: the landowning oligarchy was completely successful in neutralising democratic interpellations, and in no case did popular resistance reach the point of populist radicalisation. The reason lies in the success of the incorporation of Argentina into the world market and the great redistributive capacity of the landowning oligarchy during the expansive cycle of differential rent. I have discussed economic aspects of this process elsewhere.[27] What is important for the present purpose is that two

[26] This does not mean that the federal groups from the interior counterposed an alternative programme of economic development based on industrial sovereignty to the programme of capitalist expansion based on the penetration of imperialist capital and the full incorporation of Argentina in the world market. This fictive picture was the result of a reading of Argentinian history by nationalist writers after 1930, who thereby projected into the 19th century the connotative domain to which anti-liberalism was linked in their own epoch.

[27] 'Modos de Producción, Sistemas Económicos y Población Excedente. Aproximación Histórica a los Casos Argentino y Chileno', *Revista Latino-Americana de Sociologia*, 1969, No 2.

basic consequences followed from this process: (1) the power bloc was highly cohesive, since no sector of it either opposed the agricultural and livestock orientation of the country or was in a position to dispute oligarchic hegemony; (2) the redistributive capacity of the oligarchy enabled it to include nascent middle- and working-classes within its expansive cycle and to co-opt their respective leaderships into the power bloc. That is to say, there took place neither a crisis at the level of the power bloc nor a collapse of transformism – both of which are, as we have seen, preconditions for the emergence of populism.

It remains however, important to describe the ideological forms through which oligarchic hegemony was imposed. As we have said, this hegemony was secured in two ways: the absorption of popular interpellations into its discourse and the articulation of the ideologies which were formally in opposition to it in a peculiar form which neutralised them. Let us consider four ideological ensembles: (a) oligarchic ideology as such; (b) the ideology of the Radical Party; (c) ideologies of non-liberal oligarchies; (d) working class ideologies.

(a) *The ideology of the oligarchy as such.* To the extent that liberalism, as the oligarchic ideology, progressively asserted its hegemony, it increased its capacity for absorbing within its discourse popular-democratic interpellations which had initially been completely excluded from it. The most complete ideological expression of liberalism in its pure state, that is to say, in so far as it presented only the four previously defined coordinates and included no mass popular-democratic interpellations in its discourse, was *Mitrism.* This was the political discourse of the Buenos Aires oligarchy at a stage when its ideological hegemony over the rest of the country was minimal, when it had to assert its power by means of straightforward repression. (This was the epoch of the Paraguayan War, the confrontations with Urquiza and the federalism of Entre Rios, and the final Montonero rebellions of the interior.) Later, when the country was pacified and its economic transformation was under way, liberalism asserted its hegemony via a constant widening of the social basis of the power bloc and an increasing absorption and neutralisation of the popular-democratic ideology of the masses. The first stage of this broadening of its social base was the cooption into the power bloc of the oligarchies of the interior of the country. This process culminated in 1880 with the accession of Roca to the Presidency of the Republic. It is significant that Roca, in his partial confrontation with the Mitrism of Buenos Aires, had to incorporate into his discourse elements of the federal ideological tradition in order to differentiate himself from the latter. 'I have my traces of federalism', he said. This is a constant that was to persist throughout the history of liberal Argentina: each time the social bases of the system were widened, the new sectors co-opted into the power bloc asserted their relatively more 'democratic' character, through ideological symbols deriving from popular federal tradition.[28] Liberalism, precisely because of its increasing hegemony, could present itself as an articulating alternative to those popular interpellations it originally had excluded. Finally, the installation of electoral machines with a clientelist base definitively consecrated the new method of incorporating the masses into the system: popular traditions were accepted as a specific subculture of the dominated classes, as a *sermo humilis* disconnected from the language of power. The link between the two was provided by the local caudillo, who ; presenting himself as the intermediary between the masses and the State – established at once the unity and the chasm between them.

(b) *The ideology of the Radical Party.* The experience of Roquism presents us with this apparent paradox: liberalism was the more hegemonic to the extent that the ideological discourse of which it constituted the articulating principle was less *exclusively* liberal. The reason is, as we have said, that hegemony does not consist in the imposition of a uniform ideology but in the articulation of dissimilar ideological elements.[29] This is even clearer in the case of Irigoyen and the

[28] This does not mean that Roca was not a perfect liberal, as much as, or more than Mitre. The difference was that Roca represented a more advanced moment of liberalism, when its increasing hegemony enabled it to begin partially absorbing elements of the federal tradition and integrating them into its discourse. But of course, it would be utterly mistaken to suppose that for this reason Roca embodied a more nationalist economic policy or a greater degree of resistance to imperialist penetration.

[29] Cf. supra, p. 161.

Radical Party, in which there was a perfect synthesis between liberalism and democracy. With their cooption into the power bloc – the highest point of oligarchic transformism – popular-democratic interpellations ceased to be a subculture mediated by clientelistic machines and became incorporated into national political life. The *sermo humilis* took possession of the language of power. It was precisely this violation of the rule of the separation of styles that oligarchic liberalism felt as an outrage; hence the numerous invectives against Irigoyen which ranged from derogatory references to the 'bully-boy of Balvanera' to 'mazorquero' (member of Rosas' death squads) or even 'fascist'. Was this, therefore, a populist experience? It seems clear that it was not. The most noticeable feature of Irigoyen's political discourse, in common with other middle class reformers in Latin America during this period – Batlle y Ordoñez in Uruguay, Alessandri in Chile, Madero in Mexico, Ruy Barbosa in Brazil and Alfonso Lopez in Colombia – was undoubtedly the increasing presence within it of popular-democratic elements; but these elements remained at the emotional or rhetorical level and were never articulated as a coherent totality in opposition to liberal ideology. As we have seen, it is only this kind of articulation which gives a populist character to the presence of democratic interpellations in any given discourse. The general proposals of the middle-class reformers of this period, on the contrary, never went beyond institutional demands that accepted the liberal framework of the regime: 'my programme is the National Constitution' (Irigoyen); 'effective suffrage and no re-election' (Madero). This kind of articulation of democratic ideology is characteristic of the stage of *popular parties* and in no circumstance does it lead to populist jacobinisation.[30]

[30] By contrast, in some cases where it was more difficult for the power bloc to co-opt the middle classes and transformism operated inadequately, there occurred a jacobinisation of democratic interpellations and the emergence, even in this period, of populism. This was the case in Chile, where the collapse of Alessandri's attempts during the 20's to carry out his programme of democratic reforms within the framework of the liberal State, led to the popular dictatorship of General Ibanez, which did carry it out within a clearly nationalist and populist ideological framework. It was also the case in Peru, where the inability of oligarchic liberalism to incorporate and neutralise middle class demands led to their increasing fusion with an indigenist ideology in the APRA.

(c) *Non-liberal oligarchic ideologies.* What existed in this period in the way of a systematic attempt to create a coherent anti-liberal ideology was the very opposite of populism: it was a right-wing nationalism, emphasising whatever was authoritarian, elitist, clerical and anti-popular in the anti-liberal tradition. This ideological trend reflected, from an opposite perspective, the very high degree of fusion between democracy and liberalism in Argentina: because its exponents despised democracy and the 'radical scum', *and saw them as an inevitable result of liberalism*, they defended an authoritarian state which found its source of inspiration in Maurras. Later, on the eve of the 1930 revolution, a new element was incorporated into this tradition: *militarism* – for the role of the Army was now to transform itself, in the theories of right-wing nationalism, into the historical agent of an anti-liberal revolution. Where did this anti-liberal oligarchic ideology find its raw materials? Obviously, in the same federal traditions from which had grown popular-democratic ideologies. But, whilst the latter represented a transformation of those traditions, reducing them to a complex of symbols and ideological elements expressing the resistance of the masses to the State, oligarchic anti-liberalism effected a transformation in the opposite direction: it reduced those traditions to the ideological forms which articulated the discourse of the dominant classes before the expansion of the liberal State: clericalism, hispanicism, the continuity of colonial values and authoritarianism.

(d) *Working-class ideologies.* The most notable feature of the ideological structure of the working class of the epoch was that it made not the slightest effort to articulate popular-democratic interpellations into its political discourse. Three reasons combine to explain this phenomenon: (1) Due to the principally agrarian character of Argentina, the working class was confined to small enclaves in the big coastal cities. During this period workers were therefore marginal to the broader confrontations in which 'the people' as such was

---

Finally, it was the case too in Mexico, where the contradiction between the peasant communities and the expansion of agrarian capitalism prevented the revolution against the Porfiriato from being kept at the mere level of reforms within the liberal State, and led on the contrary to the collapse of the Madero regime and to the long process of the Mexican Revolution.

constituted. (2) The working class of this period was recruited overwhelmingly from European immigrants. This had two consequences: firstly, the fusion between their class ideology and the popular-democratic ideology of the country to which they had come, could not but be a slow process; secondly, those aspects of their new country which seemed most comprehensible in terms of their European experience were precisely the liberal State and its institutions. Hence their tendency to interpret any incomprehensible element in terms of European paradigms as the residue of a more primitive cultural stage which material progress, the expansion of the liberal State and the progressive Europeanisation of the country, would finally eliminate. The condensation of these three elements – Europeanism, liberalism and material progress – into a unified ideological discourse reproduced the kind of articulation which, as we have seen, characterised oligarchic liberalism. (3) To this it is necessary to add the specific way in which the strictly populist element was integrated into this ideology. As we know, the most characteristic structural feature of socialist ideology at the end of the 19th century and the beginning of the 20th was class reductionism, which confined the proletariat to a pure class ideology that viewed any popular interpellation as the ideology of a class enemy. Naturally this obstructed any form of socialist populism. *What is important is that this class reductionism, applied by the immigrant working class in Argentinian society, came to identify the diffuse democratic ideology of the masses as pre-capitalist residues which the progressive Europeanisation of Latin American societies would finally eliminate.* Hence the close and increasing unity between hegemonic liberal ideology and socialist ideology. The Socialist Party reasoned in the following way: the full development of a capitalist society is the precondition for the full development of the working class; therefore, the expansion of the liberal State – considered as the necessary political superstructure of capitalism – was a progressive process and must be supported. In turn it was thought that the immigration process was casting onto Argentinian shores an ever greater number of immigrants, who would in the end eliminate the ideological residues of federal and Montonera Argentina. In this way, socialist ideology accepted the articulative ensemble characteristic of liberal discourse and added only one element: working class reductionism. This element did not significantly alter the picture, however, since the working class was regarded as the social force which would carry liberal society to its democratic consummation. The Communist Party, for its part, effected an equally liberal reading of Argentinian politics – if with a different terminology. During the period of the Popular Fronts it was to measure the progressive character of different bourgeois political forces according to the degree of their adherence to liberal ideology, while denouncing as fascist any attempt to incorporate elements of popular nationalist tradition into political discourse. If we compare Argentinian socialism and communism we have to conclude, therefore, that the alternative of reform/revolution did not provide a measure of the degree of progressiveness of either ideology, since all variants of that alternative occurred within an ideological discourse which accepted all the constitutive articulations of oligarchic liberalism.

An analysis of these four ideological ensembles – which of course were not the only ones present – enables us to understand the system of ideological alternatives in pre-Peronist Argentina: an increasing unity between liberalism and democracy in the dominant discourse, a marginal authoritarian ideology, *both* anti-democratic *and* anti-liberal; class reductionism in working class ideologies. These three aspects, *taken as a whole* expressed oligarchic hegemony.

The decade of the 1930's saw important changes in this ideological crystallisation, presaging the decline of oligarchic hegemony and the emergence of new contradictions in the power bloc. In the first place, the power bloc experienced a deep crisis: the world depression led to a process of import-substituting industrialisation that created new antagonisms between nascent industrial sectors and the landowning oligarchy. Secondly, there was a crisis of transformism. As a result of the economic depression, the oligarchy could no longer tolerate the generous redistributive policies characteristic of the Radical governments, and had to ban the middle classes from access to political power. In order to do this, it established a parliamentary system based on electoral fraud. The democratic demands of the masses and the ideological symbols which represented them were less and less absorbed by the liberal regime, to a point where the scission between liberalism and democracy became complete. This was reflected in an increasing division within the Radical Party: the official party leadership, in the hands of Alvear, hoped for an impossible return of the unity between liberalism and democracy, and to this end negotiated with the now fraudulent liberal regime; it accepted subordinate positions within it to such a point that, towards the end of the period, official Radicalism was to all intents and purposes indistinguishable from the conservative coalition in power. On the other hand, a minority nationalist current tried to develop within Radicalism all the antagonism implicit in popular interpellations, to accentuate the incompatibility of liberalism and democracy, and to indict the liberal regime as a whole. English imperialism was denounced for the first time as a dominant structural force in Argentinian history; liberalism was perceived as the political superstructure necessary for the subjection of the country to the agrarian oligarchy and foreign interests; the basis was laid for a popular and anti-liberal revisionism of Argentinian history. The decade of the 1940's thus challenged Radicalism with the disarticulation of its tradition political discourse: it now had to opt for liberalism *or* democracy. The perfect synthesis between the two which had characterised Irigoyenism was dissolved.

Right-wing nationalism also underwent important changes. The implantation of an oligarchic liberal regime, which had buried their corporativist hopes, made right-wing nationalists think increasingly of an alternative military solution; the corrupt character of the conservative regime and its servile subjection to Great Britain led them to denounce imperialism; while the need to break imperialist links and to transform Argentina into an independent power led some nationalist sectors to demand an industrialist reorientation of the economy. These two new components of authoritarian nationalism – anti-imperialism and industrialism – implied a growing confrontation with oligarchic liberalism. It also presented right-wing nationalism in the 1940's with a clear alternative: either to accentuate the anti-imperialist and industrialist character of its programme which – given the increasing opposition to the latter on the part of the oligarchy – could only lead to a quest for support from a mass movement, and a consequent renunciation of the elitist and anti-popular elements in its ideology; or to retain those elements but at the cost of diluting the radicalism of the anti-oligarchic programme.

Finally, working-class ideologies also underwent a process of crisis in this period. Internal migrations had incorporated into industrial activity a new proletariat from the interior of the country, whose ideology was not based on the class reductionism of the old proletariat of European origin, but on a particular type of discourse in which popular-democratic interpellations were central. Meanwhile industrialisation was now transforming the role of the proletariat in the political process; from being a relatively marginal sector – as it had been in the Argentina of agriculture and livestock – it came to be the most concentrated social sector, and the backbone of all those forces interested in the expansion of the internal market and opposed to the continuation of oligarchic rule.

We can see, then, the extent to which the decline of oligarchic hegemony was reflected in a crisis of the dominant political discourse. This – as in any ideological crisis – consisted of a progressive disarticulation of the constitutive elements of that discourse. Liberalism and democracy ceased to be articulated; democratic interpellations could less and less be integrated into liberal ideology. For authoritarian nationalism, the possibility of a simultaneous anti-democratic and anti-liberal posture became increasingly problematic; there arose, particularly after anti-imperialist and industrial components had been incorporated into its discourse, a possibility previously non-existent: democratic authoritarianism. Finally, class reductionism and proletarian ideology ceased to be necessarily correlated and the possibility arose of a working class populism. This disarticulation meant, among other things, that the power bloc's ability to neutralise its contradictions with the people had diminished; in the mirror of liberal ideological forms, now broken and murky, new and unforeseen combinations were possible. This was a breach opened at the ideological level, and with it the possibility of populism. For populism in Argentina was to consist precisely in a reunification of the ensemble of interpellations that expressed opposition to the oligarchic power bloc – democracy, industrialism, nationalism, anti-imperialism; their condensation into a new historical subject; and a development of their potential antagonism towards a confrontation with the principle of oligarchic discourse itself – liberalism. The whole effort of Peronist ideology at this stage was bent towards the aim of detracting liberalism from its last links with a democratic connotative domain and presenting it as a straightforward cover for oligarchic class interests. Peron declared, in a revealing speech during the electoral campaign of 1946: 'I am, then, much more democratic than my adversaries, because I seek a real democracy whilst they defend an appearance of democracy, the external form of democracy. I seek a higher standard of living to protect the workers, even the poorest, from capitalist coercion; while the capitalists want the misery of the proletariat and its abandonment by the state to enable them to carry on their old tricks of buying and usurping ballot-papers. . . . In conclusion: Argentina cannot stagnate in the somnolent rhythm of activity to which so many who have come and lived at her expense have condemned her; Argentina must recover the firm pulse of a healthy and clean-living youth. Argentina needs the young blood of the working class.'[31]

This attempt to distinguish between liberal ideological forms and real democracy dominated the whole of Peronist discourse. Look at this claim: 'For the truth is this: in our country the real problem is not a conflict of "liberty" against "tyranny", Rosas against Urquiza, "democracy" against "totalitarianism". What lies at the root of the Argentinian drama is a contest between "social justice" and "social injustice". The fraud and corruption to which we have come is simply repugnant: it represents the greatest possible treachery against the working masses. The Communist and Socialist parties, which hypocritically present themselves as workers' parties whilst serving capitalist interests, have no qualms about carrying out electoral propaganda with the aid of cash handed over by the bosses. . . . To use a word of which they are very fond, we could say that they are the true representatives

[31] J. D. Peron, speech proclaiming his candidature, February 12th, 1946. Reproduced in M. Peña, *El Peronismo, Selección de Documentos para la Historia*, Buenos Aires, 1972, p. 10.

of continuism; but a continuism in the policy of workers' slavery and misery.'[32]

It is not our intention to study the evolution of Peronism as a movement, since we wish only to point out how the strictly populist moment in its ideology was constituted. But in any case we should note certain significant facts. Firstly, if the strictly populist element in Peronist ideology was the radicalisation of anti-liberal popular interpellations, Peronist discourse consisted not only of these interpellations but also of their articulation within a discourse which sought to confine any confrontation with the liberal oligarchy within limits imposed by the class project that defined the regime: the development of a national capitalism. Hence the antagonism of popular interpellations was permitted to develop only up to a certain point. Peronism sought to limit their explosive potential by presenting them always in articulation with other ideological elements which were anti-liberal, but were not popular – military or clerical ideology, for example. Secondly, if Peronism was undeniably successful in constituting a unified popular-democratic language at the national level, this was due to the social homogeneity of Argentina, exceptional in the Latin American context: lack of a peasantry, overwhelming predominance of the urban population, substantial development of the middle classes, development of trade-unionism throughout the country. Thirdly, the massive presence of the working class in Peronism gave it an exceptional ability to persist as a movement after the fall of the regime in 1955. Whilst other Latin American populist movements did not survive the fall of their regimes, the fact that Peronism was rooted in the working class enabled it to continue as a political force and even to extend its influence into the middle classes, radicalised in the last two decades as a result of the contradictions created by the expansion of monopoly capital. Fourthly, if the antagonism of popular interpellations developed only within the limits tolerated by the Peronist regime while it existed, it was impossible to impose these limits once Peronism was proscribed and started to reorganize its cadres from below. To the extent that Argentinian liberalism, restored in 1955, demonstrated its

[32] *Op. cit.*, p. 9.

complete inability to absorb the democratic demands of the masses and resorted more and more to repression, the potential antagonism of popular interpellations could develop to the full. Popular ideology became increasingly anti-liberal, and in the most radicalised sectors increasingly fused with socialism. 'National socialism' was the formula coined in the course of this process. The return to power of Peronism in 1973 proved that the change was irreversible: successive attempts to turn the clock back and to articulate popular-democratic ideology in a form assimilable by the bourgeoisie all failed. The regime of Isabel Peron collapsed into repressive chaos without having achieved any stable form of articulation between popular interpellations and bourgeois ideology.

The singularities of Peronism can be more clearly seen if we compare it with the other major populist experience in Latin America of this period, to which it is often likened: Varguism. Let us recall its origins. The Brazilian revolution of 1930 was the product of an accumulation of contradictions which, in the Argentinian experience, had been successively resolved. Inter-regional conflicts had ceased to be of decisive political importance in Argentina after the federalisation of Buenos Aires in 1880. The accession to power of the middle classes with their redistributive projects within the agro-exporting system had occurred with the electoral victory of Radicalism in 1916. The new contradictions between the agrarian and industrial sectors only became important after 1930. We find in Brazil, on the contrary, that these contradictions had not been resolved and that they accumulated in the revolutionary process of 1930. Inter-regional conflicts, in which less influential states opposed the increasing predominance of São Paolo, played a decisive role in the alliance which carried Vargas to power. The Brazilian middle classes, due to the extreme regionalisation of the country, had not been able to create a political party with national dimensions as Irigoyen had done in Argentina. The result was that they could not prevail against the political machines of the local oligarchies – witness the fruitless attempt of Ruy Barbosa in the presidential elections of 1910 – and no internal democratisation of the liberal regime took place, as had occurred in Argentina or Uruguay. These frustrated liberal-democratic tendencies – perfectly represented by the Democratic Party in São Paolo – also played an important part in the revolution. Finally, the *tenentes* were of prime importance in the seizure of power – radicalised sectors of the Army which sought to carry out a programme of democratisation and modernisation of the country, via a complete break from the oligarchical political system and the liberal State. It was in these sectors that we can find the first traces of a populist ideology.

Vargas had to manoeuvre amidst a highly complex coalition of contradictory forces, and only in 1937 was he able to establish full political control through the Estado Novo. But even then, and throughout his entire political career, Vargas was never able to become the leader of a unified and homogeneous movement like that of Peron: on the contrary, he was always to be an articulator of heterogeneous forces over which he established his personal control through a complicated system of alliances. If in the more industrialised areas of the country he was able to establish firm bases of independent support in the working class and vast sectors of the middle classes, in the interior of the country he had to seek his support from traditional political machines. This fragmentation of his political support was reflected in his inability to form a unified political party: the forces which rallied to him were organised in two parties. The Social Democratic Party (PSD) grouped the conservative forces in his coalition; the Brazilian Labour Party (PTB) was based on urban sectors, especially the working-class, and attempted to develop a populist Jacobinism. The dual face of Varguism – accentuated by the fact that the importance of the working-class in Brazil was incomparably less than in Argentina – was reflected in an inadequate and fragmented populism, which did not succeed in constituting a political language of national dimensions. Varguism was never, therefore genuinely populist. On the contrary, it oscillated in a pendular movement: at moments of stability its political language tended to be paternalistic and conservative; at moments of crisis on the other hand, when the conservative elements abandoned the coalition, it swung in a 'populist' direction – that is to say, one that developed the antagonism latent in democratic interpellations. But precisely in these crises an elementary political logic imposed itself: the social bases for a populist discourse have always so far been insufficient in Brazil to guarantee political power. This was to be demonstrated by the fate of Vargas in 1945, 1954 and finally by the fall of Goulart in 1964.

We may conclude this section by indicating why populist experiences have been less frequent in Latin America in the last two decades. I think the reasons lie in the following factors:

(a) Transformism has entered into a definitive crisis. The capacity of Latin American power blocs restructured under the hegemony of monopoly capital to absorb the democratic demands of the masses is extremely limited. I will not enter into an analysis of the economic origins of this phenomenon, which I have explored elsewhere.[33] Its consequence, in any case, is that today the dominant blocs do not even attempt to take popular initiatives – that is to say, to articulate popular-democratic ideology into the discourse of power. On the contrary, the new type of military regime in contemporary Latin America tends to rest more and more exclusively upon its repressive apparatuses. The result has been to throw into crisis not only the various populist experiences, but also the limited transformism needed for the minimal subsistence of a liberal regime. This also explains why despite the increasing authoritarianism of Latin American military regimes, they have not been able to assume in a fascist orientation for, as we have seen, the ideological base of fascism was a peculiar articulation of popular ideologies, whilst the orientation of current military dictatorships in Latin America seem to preclude *any* such articulation in its discourse.

(b) In the past a crisis of transformism led, as we have seen, to the creation of various forms of populism by dissident fractions of the dominant power bloc. Any development in this direction now, however, seems improbable for the following reasons. In the 1930's and 1940's, the power blocs were deeply divided due to the crisis of oligarchic hegemony, and at least a fraction of them was ready to move in the direction of a national independent capitalism and to seek mass support to this end.

[33] Cf. Ernesto Laclau, 'Argentina: Imperialist Strategy and the May Crisis', *New Left Review*, No 62, July–August, 1970.

Today, on the contrary, the nationalist experiences have collapsed and the power blocs have been reunited under the control of monopoly capital. In these conditions, there are no antagonisms sufficiently deep for a fraction of the power bloc to reorient in a populist direction. The second reason for thinking that a new populism of the dominant classes is unlikely is that, in the course of the experiences of the last twenty-five years, the Latin American masses have developed the antagonism inherent in democratic interpellations to a point where it is very difficult for any fraction of the bourgeoisie to absorb and neutralise them. This has led, in turn, to a consolidation of the power blocs and an accentuation of their repressive policies towards the dominated classes. For the latter, however, a new, long-term ideological perspective is opening up: to develop the radicalisation of popular-democratic ideology and increasingly fuse it with socialist ideology, at a stage when the bourgeoisie as a whole is more and more engulfed in repression and barbarism.

IV

Finally, let us point out some conclusions which follow from our analysis. 'Populism' arises in a specific ideological domain: that constituted by the double articulation of political discourse. The dialectical tension between 'the people' and classes determines the *form* of ideology, both among dominant and dominated sectors. The *metamorphoses* of 'the people' consist in its various forms of articulation with classes. To the extent that 'the people' and classes constitute poles of contradictions which are different but equally constitutive of political discourse, they are both present in it. But whilst the class contradiction determines the articulating principle of that discourse, lending it its specific singularity in a determinate ideological domain, the first contradiction represents an abstract moment which can be articulated to the most divergent class discourses. 'Populism', as a particular inflexion of popular interpellations, can never constitute the articulating principle of a political discourse – even when it constitutes a feature present in it. It is precisely this abstract character of 'populism' which permits of its presence in the ideology of the most varied of classes. The same can be said of a concept such as 'market economy', which does not define the articulating principle of an economic system – this always lies in its dominant mode of production – but which is an abstract element present in many modes of production, from slavery to capitalism, that yet constitute an indispensible component for understanding the functioning of the system as a whole.

It might be asked why, if popular-democratic ideologies do not exist separately from but are articulated within class discourses, we cannot proceed directly to a study of the latter as such, and leave aside an analysis of the former. The answer is that such an emphasis would eliminate what is most specific to the ideological class struggle – the attempt to articulate the same interpellations in antagonistic discourses. It is precisely because 'the people' can never be totally absorbed by any class discourse, because there is always a certain openness in the ideological domain, whose structuring is never complete, that the class struggle can also occur as ideological struggle. To suppose, on the contrary, that class ideologies constitute a closed and perfectly consistent bloc is to reduce the conflict between them to a purely mechanical clash which could hardly be characterised as 'ideological struggle'. To deny the dialectic between 'the people' and classes would be, then, to deny the ideological class struggle.

Let us consider more closely this characteristic dialectic between 'the people' and classes. Classes only exist as hegemonic forces to the extent that they can articulate popular interpellations to their own discourse. For the dominant classes this articulation consists, as we have seen, in a neutralisation of 'the people'. For the dominated classes to win hegemony, they must precipitate a crisis in the dominant ideological discourse and reduce its articulating principles to vacuous entelechies without any connotative power over popular interpellations. For this, they must develop the implicit antagonism of the latter to the point where 'the people' is completely unassimilable by any fraction of the power bloc. But, to present popular interpellations in the form of antagonism is, as we know, a characteristic of populism. If therefore a dominated class is to impose its hegemony through a confrontation with the power bloc, and if this confrontation necessitates the development of the antagonism implicit in popular interpellations, it can be deduced that the more radical is its confrontation with the system, the less possible will it be for that class to assert its hegemony without 'populism'. Populism is therefore not an expression of the ideological backwardness of a dominated class but, on the contrary, an expression of the moment when the articulating power of this class imposes itself hegemonically on the rest of society. This is the first movement in the dialectic between 'the people' and classes: *classes cannot assert their hegemony without articulating the people in their discourse*; *and the specific form of this articulation in the case of a class which seeks to confront the power bloc as a whole, in order to assert its hegemony, will be populism.*

Now let us look at the process from the other angle. The 'people'/power bloc contradiction cannot be developed without classes. If classes cannot be hegemonic without articulating 'the people', 'the people' only exist articulated to classes. The degree of 'populism', therefore, will depend on the nature of the antagonism existing between the class which is struggling for hegemony and the power bloc. Let us begin by posing an extreme case: that of a class which in order to assert its hegemony, demands the *full* development of the antagonism inherent in popular-democratic interpellations. What does this *full* development mean? As we have argued here – and as Badiou and Balmès have noted from a different viewpoint – to the extent that popular resistance exerts itself against a power external and opposed to 'the people', that is to say, *against the very form of the State*, the resolution of 'the people'/power bloc contradiction can only consist in the suppression of the State as an antagonistic force with respect to the people. Therefore, the only social sector which can aspire to the full development of 'the people'/power bloc contradiction, that is to say, *to the highest and most radical form of populism*, is that whose *class interests* lead it to the suppression of the State as an antagonistic force. *In socialism*, *therefore*, *coincide the highest form of 'populism' and the resolution of the ultimate and most radical of class conflicts*. The dialectic between 'the people' and classes finds here the final moment of its unity: there is no socialism without populism, and the highest forms of populism can only be socialist. This is the profound intuition present from Mao to Togliatti in all those trends within Marxism which, from very diverse political positions and cultural traditions, have tried to go beyond class reductionism. The advance towards socialism can only consist, in that sense, in a long series of struggles through which socialism asserts its popular identity and 'the people' its socialist objectives. Socialist hegemony does not mean the pure and simple destruction of the previous society, but the absorption of its elements into a new articulation. It is only when socialism has developed this articulating capacity that it comes to be hegemonic.

Let us consider the opposite situation: that in which populism is developed by a class whose antagonism against the power bloc is less radical and which does not lead to the suppression of the State as an antagonistic force with regard to 'the people'. The dialectic between the people and classes leads in this case to different forms of articulation. The feature common to them all is that populist radicalisation of democratic interpellations must be linked to a connotative domain of such a kind as to contain the antagonism implicit in popular-democratic interpellations within the limits necessary for the confrontation of the new dominant class with the traditional power bloc. We already know how this neutralisation was achieved in the case of fascism: popular interpellations were linked to contents such as racism and corporativism which obstructed their radicalisation in a socialist direction. We also know that the maintenance of these limits necessitates a high degree of ideological homogenisation which was made possible only by repression. Hence the 'totalitarian' character of fascism. In the case of Bonapartist regimes – such as Peronism – the method of neutralisation was different: it consisted essentially in allowing the persistence of various 'elites' which based their support of the regime upon antagonistic articulating projects, and in confirming state power as a mediating force between them. There was thus a coexistence in Argentina between groups basing their support for the regime upon an articulation of 'populism' and clerical anti-liberalism, 'populism' and nazism, 'populism' and trade-unionist reformism, 'populism' and democratic anti-imperialism, and finally, 'populism' and socialism. The Bonapartist state exerted a mediating power between these opposed bases of support and coalesced very few ideological symbols. The renowned ideological poverty and lack of official doctrine of Peronism is to be explained precisely by this mediating character of the State and Peron himself. Fascism, on the other hand, could develop a more precise official doctrine and a more defined ideological structure to the extent that it was a less 'mediating' and more 'totalitarian' experience. Bonapartist régimes, by definition, do not seek a unification or assimilation of ideological apparatuses, since it is precisely in their mediating capacity between opposing forces that their source of power is to be found. It is for this reason that, as we have pointed out, the radicalisation of Peronist political language beyond the limits tolerable to Bonapartism was a process that occurred after the fall of Peronism in 1955.

To conclude, we must answer the following question: why not limit the use of the term 'populism' to the second case we have analysed, and adopt a different terminology to refer to those experiences where radicalised popular interpellations have been articulated with socialism? This would apparently be the most sensible course, given the pejorative connotations generally associated with the term 'populism' I do not think, however, that such a decision would be appropriate for it would obscure the universality of the basic premise constituted by the dual articulation of political discourse, and could lead to the illusion that popular interpellations within socialist discourse were *created* by this discourse and were absent from the ideology of dominant classes. This would be the surest way of falling into class reductionism. On the contrary, to assert the relative continuity of popular interpellations by contrast with the discontinuous articulations of class discourses, is the only valid starting point for a scientific study of political ideologies.

Index